Second Workshop on Advances in Text Input Methods

(WTIM 2)

Held at the 24th International Conference on Computational Linguistics (COLING 2012)

Mumbai, India
15 December 2012

Editors:

Kalika Bali
Monojit Choudhury
Yoh Okuno

ISBN: 978-1-62748-349-0

Printed from e-media with permission by:

Curran Associates, Inc.
57 Morehouse Lane
Red Hook, NY 12571

Some format issues inherent in the e-media version may also appear in this print version.

Printed by Curran Associates, Inc. (2013)

For permission requests, please contact the Association for Computational Linguistics at the address below.

Association for Computational Linguistics
209 N. Eighth Street
Stroudsburg, Pennsylvania 18360

Phone: 1-570-476-8006
Fax: 1-570-476-0860

acl@aclweb.org

Additional copies of this publication are available from:

Curran Associates, Inc.
57 Morehouse Lane
Red Hook, NY 12571 USA
Phone: 845-758-0400
Fax: 845-758-2634
Email: curran@proceedings.com
Web: www.proceedings.com

COLING 2012

24th International Conference on Computational Linguistics

Proceedings of the Second Workshop on Advances in Text Input Methods (WTIM 2)

Workshop chairs:
Kalika Bali, Monojit Choudhury and Yoh Okuno

15 December 2012
Mumbai, India

Preface

It is our great pleasure to present the proceedings of the Second Workshop on Advances in Text Input Methods (WTIM-2) held in conjunction with Coling 2012, on 15th December 2012, in Mumbai, India. This workshop is a sequel to the first WTIM which was held in conjunction with IJCNLP 2011 in November 2011, Chiang Mai, Thailand. The aim of the current workshop remains the same as the previous one that is to bring together the researchers and developers of text input technologies around the world, and share their innovations, research findings and issues across different applications, devices, modes and languages.

The proceedings contain nine contributions, five as long papers and the rest as short papers or demonstration proposals. Together they cover research on various languages including Assamese, Arabic, Bangla, Chinese, Dzongkha and Japanese, as well as keyboard design aspects of many languages using Brahmi derived scripts. The workshop featured two invited talks by Paul Butcher, Chief Software Architect of SwiftKey and Ram Prakash H., Founder and CEO of Tachyon Technologies, both of whom gave insights into development and deployment of commercial text input systems SwiftKey and Quillpad respectively. We would like to thank both the speakers for taking the time to share their experiences. The volume also includes a paper by Ram Prakash H. based on his invited talk.

In order to facilitate more interaction between the participants and presenters, all papers in WTIM-2 were presented as posters during a long session, which was preceded by short elevator pitches. In line with the same objective of increased interaction, we organized two focused sessions namely an open discussion on data and resources and a panel discussion on research and community building for text input methods.

We would like to take this opportunity to thank all the panelists, participants, presenters and authors for making WTIM-2 an enriching experience. We would also like to thank our PC members who did a wonderful job of critically reviewing the submissions and providing constructive feedback to the authors. Thanks are also due to Coling 2012 organizers for giving us this opportunity and helping us with various phases of organization, and to Microsoft Research Lab India for sponsorship. Last but not the least we would like to extend our gratitude to Hisami Suzuki, Microsoft, the founding co-chair of WTIM series, who advised us on different aspects of organization of the workshop.

Kalika Bali, Monojit Choudhury, Yoh Okuno
Organizing Co-Chairs
WTIM 2012

Committees

Organizing Co-chairs

Kalika Bali, Microsoft Research Lab India
Monojit Choudhury, Microsoft Research Lab India
Yoh Okuno, SwiftKey

Program Committee

Achraf Chalabi, Microsoft ATLC, Egypt
Hiroshi Manabe
Hiroyuki Tokunaga, Preferred Infrastructure
Hisami Suzuki, Microsoft Research Lab Redmond
Jugal Kalita, University of Colorado, Colorado Springs
Jun Hatori, Apple
Pushpak Bhattacharyya, IIT Bombay
Richa, LDC-IL, Central Institute of Indian Languages Mysore
Samit Bhattacharya, IIT Guwahati
Sarvnaz Karimi, CSIRO, Sydney
Shinsuke Mori, Kyoto University
Sriganesh Madhvanath, HP Labs India
Taku Kudo, Google Japan
Tim Paek, Microsoft Research Lab Redmond
Vasudeva Varma, IIIT Hyderabad
Virach Sornlertlamvanich, NECTEC
Xianchao Wu, Baidu

Invited Talks

SwiftKey: Building a commercial success upon firm theoretical foundations

Speaker: *Paul Butcher, SwiftKey*

Abstract: At the heart of SwiftKey's success are well motivated Machine Learning and Natural Language Processing principles. But that foundation is only the start, it's also required relentless focus on User Experience, solving endless real world issues and building and connecting with the vibrant community of SwiftKey users worldwide. This talk will take you through the story of how we turned a great IME into the most successful paid Android application in the world.

Speaker's Bio: Paul is Chief Software Architect of NLP company SwiftKey, creators of the market-leading input method by the same name.

Quillpad multilingual predictive transliteration system

Speaker: *Ram Prakash H, Tachyon Technologies*

Abstract: Transliteration has been one of the common methods for multilingual text input. Many earlier methods employed transliteration schemes for defining one to one mapping of input alphabet combinations to output alphabet combinations. Though such well-defined mappings made it easier to write a transliteration program, the end user was burdened with learning the mappings. Further, though transliteration schemes try to map the alphabet combinations phonetically, it is unavoidable to introduce non intuitive combinations into the scheme. An alternative is to use predictive transliteration, where user could input a word, by intuitively combining the input alphabet phonetically and the predictive transliteration system should correctly convert it to the target language. In this talk, I will present the challenges that must be addressed by such a system, and describe how Quillpad can be trained for performing predictive transliteration between any two alphabets.

Speaker's Bio: Ram Prakash is the founder of Tachyon Technologies, and developer of Quillpad, the first online Indian language phonetic transliteration based input system. He was listed as one of the twenty MIT TR-35 2010 Young Innovators from India for Quillpad.

Table of Contents

Second Workshop on Advances in Text Input Methods (WTIM 2)

Program

Saturday, 15 December 2012

0900-09:10	Welcome Address by the Organizing Co-chairs
09:10–10:00	**Invited Talk** *SwiftKey: Building a commercial success upon firm theoretical foundations* Paul Butcher, SwiftKey
	Poster Boasters
10:00–10:12	*Statistical Input Method based on a Phrase Class n-gram Model* Hirokuni Maeta and Shinsuke Mori
10:12–10:24	*An Ensemble Model of Word-based and Character-based Models for Japanese and Chinese Input Method* Yoh Okuno and Shinsuke Mori
10:24–10:36	*Multi-objective Optimization for Efficient Brahmic Keyboards* Albert Brouillette, Devraj Sarmah and Jugal Kalita
10:36–10:48	*Using Collocations and K-means Clustering to Improve the N-pos Model for Japanese IME* Long Chen, Xianchao Wu and Jingzhou He
10:48–11:00	*phloat : Integrated Writing Environment for ESL learners* Yuta Hayashibe, Masato Hagiwara and Satoshi Sekine
11:00–11:05	*Bangla Phonetic Input Method with Foreign Words Handling* Khan Md. Anwarus Salam, Nishino Tetsuro and Setsuo Yamada
11:05–11:10	*LuitPad: A fully Unicode compatible Assamese writing software* Navanath Saharia and Kishori M. Konwar
11:10–11:15	*Romanized Arabic Transliteration* Achraf Chalabi and Hany Gerges
11:15–11:30	*Forward Transliteration of Dzongkha Text to Braille* Tirthankar Dasgupta, Manjira Sinha and Anupam Basu
11:30–12:00	Coffee break
12:00–12:45	*Quillpad Multilingual Predictive Transliteration System* Ram Prakash H
	Open Discussion
12:45–13:30	Data and Resources for Research on Text Input Methods
13:30–14:30	Lunch

Saturday, 15 December 2012 (continued)

	Poster and Demo Session
14:30–16:00	All long, short and demo paper will be presented as posters for better interaction among the participants and presenters
16:00–16:30	Coffee break
	Panel Discussion
16:30–17:45	Future of Text Input Systems: Research directions and community building
17:45	Vote of Thanks and Closing

Statistical Input Method based on a Phrase Class n-gram Model

Hirokuni Maeta[1] *Shinsuke Mori*[1]
(1) Graduate School of Informatics, Kyoto University, Yoshida Honmachi, Sakyo-ku, Kyoto, Japan
maeta@ar.media.kyoto-u.ac.jp, forest@i.kyoto-u.ac.jp

ABSTRACT
We propose a method to construct a phrase class n-gram model for Kana-Kanji Conversion by combining phrase and class methods. We use a word-pronunciation pair as the basic prediction unit of the language model. We compared the conversion accuracy and model size of a phrase class bi-gram model constructed by our method to a tri-gram model. The conversion accuracy was measured by F measure and model size was measured by the vocabulary size and the number of non-zero frequency entries. The F measure of our phrase class bi-gram model was 90.41%, while that of a word-pronunciation pair tri-gram model was 90.21%. In addition, the vocabulary size and the number of non-zero frequency entries in the phrase class bi-gram model were 5,550 and 206,978 respectively, while those of the tri-gram model were 22,801 and 645,996 respectively. Thus our method makes a smaller, more accurate language model.

KEYWORDS: Kana-Kanji Conversion, n-gram model, phrase-based model, class-based model.

1 Introduction

Japanese input methods are an essential technology for Japanese computing. Japanese has over 6,000 characters, which is much larger than the number of keys in a keyboard. It is impossible to map each Japanese character to a key. So an alternate input method for Japanese characters is needed. This is done by inputting a pronunciation sequence and converting it to an output sequence of words. Here, the input sequence of pronunciation is a sequence of *kana* characters and the output sequence of words is a mixture of *kana* and *kanji* characters. So this conversion is called *Kana-Kanji Conversion* (KKC).

The noisy channel model approach has been successfully applied to input methods (Chen and Lee, 2000; Mori et al., 1999). In KKC, a word sequence is predicted from a pronunciation sequence. The system is composed of two modules: a language model, which measures the likelihood of a word sequence in the language and a word-pronunciation model, which describes a relationship between a word sequence and a pronunciation sequence. Thus, the conversion accuracy of KKC depends on the language model and the word-pronunciation model. The language model is, however, more important since it describes the context and it is larger in size than the word-pronunciation model.

We focus on how to improve the language model for KKC. An n-gram model is generally used for many tasks. In KKC, considering the need for the conversion speed and the size of the language model, bi-gram models are often used. However, bi-gram models can not refer to a long history. A tri-gram model, which is also popular for many tasks, can refer a longer history but the size of tri-gram models is larger than that of bi-gram models. There have been many attempts at improving language models. A class n-gram model (Brown et al., 1992; Kneser and Ney, 1993; Mori et al., 1998), which groups words of similar behavior into a single class, and a phrase n-gram model (Deligne and Bimbot, 1995; Ries et al., 1996; Mori et al., 1997) which replaces some word sequences by single tokens, are known to be practical in speech recognition community.

In this paper, we propose a method to construct a smaller, more accurate language model for KKC. It is often thought that accurate models are larger and that small models are less accurate. However, we successfully built a smaller, more accurate language model. This is done by combining phrase and class methods. First, we collect phrases and construct a phrase sequence corpus. By changing the prediction unit from a word to a word sequence, the model can use a longer history. Then we perform word clustering to restrict the growth of the model size. As a result, we obtain a phrase class n-gram model. This model is small and expected to be accurate because it uses a history as long as those used by higher order n-gram models.

In order to test the effectiveness of our method, we compared the conversion accuracy and the model size of the phrase class bi-gram model constructed by our method to other language models. We used a word-pronunciation pair as the basic prediction unit of the language models. The conversion accuracy is measured by F measure, which is the harmonic mean of precision and recall. The F measure of our phrase class bi-gram model was 90.41%, while that of a word-pronunciation pair tri-gram model was 90.21%. In addition, the vocabulary size and the number of non-zero frequency entries in the phrase class bi-gram model were 5,550 and 206,978 respectively, while those of the tri-gram model were 22,801 and 645,996 respectively. These results show that our method of combining phrase and class methods makes a smaller, more accurate language model for KKC.

2 Statistical Input Method

In this section we give a brief explanation of a statistical input method and a word-pronunciation pair n-gram model, which is applied as the language model to KKC in the subsequent sections.

2.1 Input Method based on a Word n-gram Model

We explain a statistical approach to an input method based on the noisy channel model (Chen and Lee, 2000; Mori et al., 1999). This approach uses a word as the prediction unit of a language model.

Let $\boldsymbol{x} = x_1 x_2 \cdots x_l$ be a pronunciation sequence and $\boldsymbol{w} = w_1 w_2 \cdots w_m$ be a word sequence. Given $\boldsymbol{x}$ as input, the goal of the input method is to output $\hat{\boldsymbol{w}}$ that maximizes the probability $p(\boldsymbol{w}|\boldsymbol{x})$ as follows:

$$\hat{\boldsymbol{w}} = \mathop{\mathbf{argmax}}_{\boldsymbol{w}} p(\boldsymbol{w}|\boldsymbol{x}).$$

By Bayes' theorem,

$$p(\boldsymbol{w}|\boldsymbol{x}) = \frac{p(\boldsymbol{x}|\boldsymbol{w})p(\boldsymbol{w})}{p(\boldsymbol{x})}.$$

Since $p(\boldsymbol{x})$ is independent of $\boldsymbol{w}$, we have

$$\begin{aligned} \hat{\boldsymbol{w}} &= \mathop{\mathbf{argmax}}_{\boldsymbol{w}} p(\boldsymbol{w}|\boldsymbol{x}) \\ &= \mathop{\mathbf{argmax}}_{\boldsymbol{w}} \frac{p(\boldsymbol{x}|\boldsymbol{w})p(\boldsymbol{w})}{p(\boldsymbol{x})} \\ &= \mathop{\mathbf{argmax}}_{\boldsymbol{w}} p(\boldsymbol{x}|\boldsymbol{w})p(\boldsymbol{w}). \end{aligned}$$

Here, the problem is divided into two parts. $p(\boldsymbol{w})$ is a language model and we call $p(\boldsymbol{x}|\boldsymbol{w})$ a word-pronunciation model.

A language model $p(\boldsymbol{w})$ outputs the probability of a word sequence $\boldsymbol{w}$. First the probability $p(\boldsymbol{w})$ is assumed to be expressed as a product of a set of conditional probabilities

$$\begin{aligned} p(\boldsymbol{w}) &= p(w_1 w_2 \cdots w_m) \\ &= \prod_{i=1}^{m} p(w_i|w_1 w_2 \cdots w_{i-1}). \end{aligned} \tag{1}$$

Then $p(w_i|w_1 \cdots w_{i-1})$ is approximated as k-order Markov process

$$p(w_i|w_1 w_2 \cdots w_{i-1}) \approx p(w_i|w_{i-k} w_{i-k+1} \cdots w_{i-1}),$$

where $k = n - 1$.

The other part, the word-pronunciation model $p(\boldsymbol{x}|\boldsymbol{w})$, outputs the probability of the pronunciation sequence $\boldsymbol{x}$ given the word sequence $\boldsymbol{w}$. This probability is assumed to be decomposed as follows:

$$p(\boldsymbol{x}|\boldsymbol{w}) = \prod_{i=1}^{m} p(\boldsymbol{x}_i|w_i),$$

where $\boldsymbol{x}_i$ is the sequence of pronunciation corresponding to the word w_i.

詰め/tsu-me 将棋/sho-u-gi の/no 本/ho-n を/wo
買/ka っ/ttsu て/te き/ki ま/ma し/shi た/ta 。/.

Figure 1: An example of a word-pronunciation pair sentence.

2.2 A Word-pronunciation Pair n-gram Model

In this paper we use a word-pronunciation pair n-gram model. A word-pronunciation pair n-gram model takes a pair of a word and its pronunciation as the prediction unit. Thus we can model a word and its pronunciation at the same time. This is because some Japanese kanji characters have the same pronunciation. So it is expected to be better to predict both a word and its pronunciation than predicting a word only.

Figure 1 shows an example of a corpus for training a word-pronunciation pair n-gram model. Units are separated with a white space. The left hand side of the slash in a unit is a word and right hand side is its pronunciation.

First we change the mathematics of the input method.

$$\begin{aligned} \hat{\boldsymbol{w}} &= \operatorname*{\mathbf{argmax}}_{\boldsymbol{w}} p(\boldsymbol{w}|\boldsymbol{x}) \\ &= \operatorname*{\mathbf{argmax}}_{\boldsymbol{w}} \frac{p(\boldsymbol{w},\boldsymbol{x})}{p(\boldsymbol{x})} \\ &= \operatorname*{\mathbf{argmax}}_{\boldsymbol{w}} p(\boldsymbol{w},\boldsymbol{x}). \end{aligned} \tag{2}$$

Here, the problem is $p(\boldsymbol{w},\boldsymbol{x})$ only. Then we express $p(\boldsymbol{w},\boldsymbol{x})$ by a word-pronunciation pair n-gram model as follows:

$$p(\boldsymbol{w},\boldsymbol{x}) = p(\langle w_1,\boldsymbol{x}_1\rangle\langle w_2,\boldsymbol{x}_2\rangle\cdots\langle w_m,\boldsymbol{x}_m\rangle),$$

where $\langle w_i,\boldsymbol{x}_i\rangle$ denotes a pair of a word w_i and its pronunciation $\boldsymbol{x}_i$. The character subsequences $\boldsymbol{x}_1$, $\boldsymbol{x}_2$, ..., $\boldsymbol{x}_m$ satisfy that

$$\boldsymbol{x} = \boldsymbol{x}_1\boldsymbol{x}_2\cdots\boldsymbol{x}_m. \tag{3}$$

A word-pronunciation pair n-gram model outputs the probability of a word-pronunciation pair sequence $\langle w_1,\boldsymbol{x}_1\rangle\langle w_2,\boldsymbol{x}_2\rangle\cdots\langle w_m,\boldsymbol{x}_m\rangle$. Like word n-gram models, this probability is expressed as a product of a set of conditional probabilities and approximated as k-order Markov process, where $k = n - 1$

$$\begin{aligned} & p(\langle w_1,\boldsymbol{x}_1\rangle\langle w_2,\boldsymbol{x}_2\rangle\cdots\langle w_m,\boldsymbol{x}_m\rangle) \\ &\quad = \prod_{i=1}^{m} p(\langle w_i,\boldsymbol{x}_i\rangle|\langle w_1,\boldsymbol{x}_1\rangle\langle w_2,\boldsymbol{x}_2\rangle\cdots\langle w_{i-1},\boldsymbol{x}_{i-1}\rangle), \\ & p(\langle w_i,\boldsymbol{x}_i\rangle|\langle w_1,\boldsymbol{x}_1\rangle\langle w_2,\boldsymbol{x}_2\rangle\cdots\langle w_{i-1},\boldsymbol{x}_{i-1}\rangle) \\ &\quad \approx p(\langle w_i,\boldsymbol{x}_i\rangle|\langle w_{i-k},\boldsymbol{x}_{i-k}\rangle\langle w_{i-k+1},\boldsymbol{x}_{i-k+1}\rangle\cdots\langle w_{i-1},\boldsymbol{x}_{i-1}\rangle). \end{aligned}$$

2.3 Parameter Estimation

The probability $p(\langle w_i, \boldsymbol{x}_i\rangle | \langle w_{i-k}, \boldsymbol{x}_{i-k}\rangle\langle w_{i-k+1}, \boldsymbol{x}_{i-k+1}\rangle \cdots \langle w_{i-1}, \boldsymbol{x}_{i-1}\rangle)$ is defined by maximum likelihood from a training corpus

$$\begin{aligned} & p(\langle w_i, \boldsymbol{x}_i\rangle | \langle w_{i-k}, \boldsymbol{x}_{i-k}\rangle\langle w_{i-k+1}, \boldsymbol{x}_{i-k+1}\rangle \cdots \langle w_{i-1}, \boldsymbol{x}_{i-1}\rangle) \\ & \stackrel{def.}{=} \frac{N(\langle w_{i-k}, \boldsymbol{x}_{i-k}\rangle\langle w_{i-k+1}, \boldsymbol{x}_{i-k+1}\rangle \cdots \langle w_{i-1}, \boldsymbol{x}_{i-1}\rangle\langle w_i, \boldsymbol{x}_i\rangle)}{N(\langle w_{i-k}, \boldsymbol{x}_{i-k}\rangle\langle w_{i-k+1}, \boldsymbol{x}_{i-k+1}\rangle \cdots \langle w_{i-1}, \boldsymbol{x}_{i-1}\rangle)}, \end{aligned}$$

where $N(\langle w, \boldsymbol{x}\rangle \cdots)$ is the number of times that the word-pronunciation pair sequence occurs in the corpus. The word segmentation and pronunciation tagging of the training corpus should be accurate.

2.4 Interpolation

There are data-sparseness problems such that a zero-probability problem. In order to avoid these problems, we use a linear interpolation (Brown et al., 1992).

$$\begin{aligned} & p'(\langle w_i, \boldsymbol{x}_i\rangle | \langle w_{i-k}, \boldsymbol{x}_{i-k}\rangle\langle w_{i-k+1}, \boldsymbol{x}_{i-k+1}\rangle \cdots \langle w_{i-1}, \boldsymbol{x}_{i-1}\rangle) \\ & = \sum_{j=0}^{k} \lambda_j p(\langle w_i, \boldsymbol{x}_i\rangle | \langle w_{i-j}, \boldsymbol{x}_{i-j}\rangle\langle w_{i-j+1}, \boldsymbol{x}_{i-j+1}\rangle \cdots \langle w_{i-1}, \boldsymbol{x}_{i-1}\rangle), \end{aligned}$$

where $0 \leq \lambda_j \leq 1$, $\sum_{j=0}^{k} \lambda_j = 1$.

2.5 Unknown Word Model

The probability $p(w, \boldsymbol{x})$ in Equation (2) equals to 0 if the input character sequence $\boldsymbol{x}$ can not be expressed as a sequence of characters in the vocabulary. In other words, in this case, the system can not find $\langle w_1, \boldsymbol{x}_1\rangle\langle w_2, \boldsymbol{x}_2\rangle \cdots \langle w_m, \boldsymbol{x}_m\rangle$ that satisfies Equation (3). So we need a model that gives the probability larger than 0 for these character sequences. This model is called an unknown word model.

An unknown word model $p(\boldsymbol{x})$ outputs the probability of a character sequence $\boldsymbol{x}$ and it should give a higher probability if the character sequence is likely a word not in a vocabulary of the language model.

As word n-gram models are often used to predict a word sequence, character n-gram models are often used to predict a character sequence of an unknown word. So $p(\boldsymbol{x})$ is easily trained from the words in a training corpus that are not in the vocabulary.

3 Language Model Improvement

Class modeling (Brown et al., 1992; Kneser and Ney, 1993; Mori et al., 1998) makes smaller language models and phrase modeling (Deligne and Bimbot, 1995; Ries et al., 1996; Mori et al., 1997) makes more accurate language models. They are known to be practical in speech recognition community. In this section we give a brief explanation of these improvements. The prediction unit of the models here is a word, but we apply these ideas to the word-pronunciation pair n-gram model for our statistical input method by changing the prediction unit.

3.1 Class n-gram Model

We use an n-gram model as the language model for KKC. An n-gram model predicts the i-th word referring to the last $n-1$ words. Although an n-gram model works well, the model size is often the serious problem.

One of the solutions to this problem is grouping similar words together. By assigning words to its class, we can obtain the language model of less states. Let f be a function that maps a word w into its class c. Given the map f, a *class n-gram model* predicts the i-th class referring to the last $k = n-1$ classes and the i-th word referring to the i-th class. Therefore we define $p(w_i|w_{i-k}w_{i-k+1}\cdots w_{i-1})$ in Equation (1) as follows:

$$p(w_i|w_{i-k}w_{i-k+1}\cdots w_{i-1}) \stackrel{def.}{=} p(c_i|c_{i-k}c_{i-k+1}\cdots c_{i-1})p(w_i|c_i),$$

where $c_* = f(w_*)$. With the map f, $p(c_i|c_{i-k}c_{i-k+1}\cdots c_{i-1})$ and $p(w_i|c_i)$ are defined by maximum likelihood from a training corpus.

$$p(c_i|c_{i-k}c_{i-k+1}\cdots c_{i-1}) \stackrel{def.}{=} \frac{N(c_{i-k}c_{i-k+1}\cdots c_{i-1}c_i)}{N(c_{i-k}c_{i-k+1}\cdots c_{i-1})}$$

$$p(w_i|c_i) \stackrel{def.}{=} \frac{N(w_i)}{N(c_i)},$$

where $N(c\cdots)$ is the number of times that the class sequence occurs in the corpus.

The problem is how to determine the map f. In other words, how to do *word clustering*. Of course it should be done carefully, or the language model would get worse.

There are some methods for word clustering. Here we follow (Mori et al., 1998)'s clustering method, where the criterion is the average cross-entropy of sub corpora. Because of this criterion, this method is expected not to increase the cross-entropy of language models.

In the method, first the training corpus is split into k sub corpora $C_1, C_2, \ldots, C_k$. Then $\{C_1, C_2, \ldots, C_k\} \setminus \{C_i\}$ is used to estimate the model parameters and C_i is used to evaluate the objective function for $i = 1, 2, \cdots, k$. The objective function is the average cross-entropy

$$\overline{H}(f) \stackrel{def.}{=} \frac{1}{k}\sum_{i=1}^{k} H(M_i(f), C_i),$$

where $M_i(f)$ is a class n-gram model constructed from f, which maps a word into its class, and sub corpora $\{C_1, C_2, \ldots, C_k\} \setminus \{C_i\}$. Thus $H(M_i(f), C_i)$ is the cross-entropy of the corpus C_i by the model $M_i(f)$ and $\overline{H}(f)$ is their average. The lower $\overline{H}(f)$ is, the better f is expected to be. This is just like evaluating a language model.

Therefore the best map $\hat{f}$ is the one that minimizes $\overline{H}(f)$. Namely,

$$\hat{f} = \mathop{\mathbf{argmin}}_{f} \overline{H}(f).$$

It is, however, impossible to find the best map among all the possible maps. Alternatively we apply a greedy algorithm, which is shown in Figure 2, to find an optimal $\hat{f}$.

Sort words $w_1, w_2, \ldots, w_N$ by frequency in descending order.
for $i \leftarrow 1, N$ **do**
    $c_i \leftarrow \{w_i\}$
    $f(w_i) \leftarrow c_i$
end for
for $i \leftarrow 2, N$ **do**
    $c \leftarrow \mathbf{argmin}_{c \in \{c_1, c_2, \ldots, c_{i-1}\}} \overline{H}(\textsc{move}(f, w_i, c))$
    if $\overline{H}(\textsc{move}(f, w_i, c)) < \overline{H}(f)$ **then**
        $f \leftarrow \textsc{move}(f, w_i, c)$
    end if
end for

procedure $\textsc{move}(f, w, c)$
    $f(w) \leftarrow f(w) \setminus \{w\}$
    $c \leftarrow c \cup f(w)$
    return f
end procedure

Figure 2: Clustering algorithm

3.2 Phrase n-gram Model

Here we explain the other language model improvement. We saw two kinds of n-gram models so far: a word n-gram model and a class n-gram model. Both models predict the next word referring to the last $n-1$ words. In other words, each of the prediction units of the models is a word. Actually, language models whose prediction unit is a word does not always have the best performance. A *phrase n-gram model*, whose prediction unit is a word sequence, can treat a word sequence that co-occurs frequently as a single word. Thus we can expect that it improves n-gram models.

The mathematics of a phrase n-gram model is the same as that of a word n-gram model except for the prediction unit because of the definition of the phrase model.

Let $\boldsymbol{w} = w_1 w_2 \cdots w_m$ be the input sequence of words. In a phrase n-gram model, the word sequence $\boldsymbol{w}$ is converted to the phrase sequence $\boldsymbol{\gamma} = \gamma_1 \gamma_2 \cdots \gamma_{m'}$ and the phrase sequence $\boldsymbol{\gamma}$ is predicted,

$$p(\boldsymbol{w}) \stackrel{def.}{=} p(\boldsymbol{\gamma}).$$

A phrase γ_i is a token that represents a word sequence. So $\boldsymbol{\gamma}$ becomes $\boldsymbol{w}$ if each phrase is replaced by its words.
Then $p(\boldsymbol{\gamma})$ is calculated like word n-gram models,

$$\begin{aligned} p(\boldsymbol{\gamma}) &= p(\gamma_1 \gamma_2 \cdots \gamma_{m'}) \\ &= \prod_{i=1}^{m'} p(\gamma_i | \gamma_1 \cdots \gamma_{i-1}), \\ p(\gamma_i | \gamma_1 \cdots \gamma_{i-1}) &\approx p(\gamma_i | \gamma_{i-k} \gamma_{i-k+1} \cdots \gamma_{i-1}), \end{aligned}$$

$\Gamma \leftarrow \{\}$
Estimate the interpolation coefficients.
Collect all the word sequences $\gamma_1, \gamma_2, \cdots, \gamma_i, \cdots$ where γ_i is a sequence of 2 or more words and it occurs in all the sub corpora C_1, C_2, ..., C_k.
Sort $\gamma_1, \cdots, \gamma_N, \gamma_{N+1}, \cdots$ so that $\overline{H}(\{\gamma_1\}) < \cdots < \overline{H}(\{\gamma_N\}) < \overline{H}(\{\}) < \overline{H}(\{\gamma_{N+1}\})$.
for $i \leftarrow 1, N$ **do**
    if $\overline{H}(\Gamma \cup \{\gamma_i\}) < \overline{H}(\Gamma)$ **then**
        $\Gamma \leftarrow \Gamma \cup \{\gamma_i\}$
        Estimate the interpolation coefficients.
    end if
end for

Figure 3: Algorithm for finding phrases

where $k = n-1$. $p(\gamma_i|\gamma_{i-k}\gamma_{i-k+1}\cdots\gamma_{i-1})$ is defined by maximum likelihood from a training corpus

$$p(\gamma_i|\gamma_{i-k}\gamma_{i-k+1}\cdots\gamma_{i-1}) \stackrel{def.}{=} \frac{N(\gamma_{i-k}\gamma_{i-k+1}\cdots\gamma_{i-1}\gamma_i)}{N(\gamma_{i-k}\gamma_{i-k+1}\cdots\gamma_{i-1})},$$

where $N(\gamma\cdots)$ is the number of times that the phrase sequence occurs in the corpus.

Phrase n-gram models require a phrase sequence corpus that can be obtained by collecting sequences of words for phrases and replacing each of those sequences in the original corpus by a single token. Sequences of words should be collected so that, by treating each of them as a single token, a phrase n-gram model has less cross-entropy.

Here we follow (Mori et al., 1997), where sequences of words are collected so that the average cross-entropy of sub corpora becomes less by the replacement of those sequences by tokens. This method find a sequence of greater than or equal to two words and it is expected to decrease the cross-entropy of language models because of the criterion.

The method of finding phrases is similar to that of word clustering. Here the training corpus is split into k sub corpora C_1, C_2, ..., C_k. $\{C_1, C_2, \ldots, C_k\} \setminus \{C_i\}$ is used to estimate the model parameters and C_i is used to evaluate the objective function for $i = 1, 2, \cdots, k$. The objective function is the average cross-entropy

$$\overline{H}(\Gamma) \stackrel{def.}{=} \frac{1}{k}\sum_{i=1}^{k} H(M_i(\Gamma), C_i),$$

where $M_i(\Gamma)$ is a phrase n-gram model constructed from a set of word sequences for phrases Γ and sub corpora $\{C_1, C_2, \ldots, C_k\} \setminus \{C_i\}$. Thus $H(M_i(\Gamma), C_i)$ is the cross-entropy of the corpus C_i by the model $M_i(\Gamma)$ and $\overline{H}(\Gamma)$ is their average. The lower $\overline{H}(\Gamma)$ is, the better Γ is expected to be.

Therefore the best set of word sequences $\hat{\Gamma}$ is the one that minimizes $\overline{H}(\Gamma)$. Namely,

$$\hat{\Gamma} = \mathop{\mathbf{argmin}}_{\Gamma} \overline{H}(\Gamma).$$

It is, however, impossible to find the best set among all the possible sets. Alternatively we apply a greedy algorithm, which is shown in Figure 3, to find an optimal $\hat{\Gamma}$.

1: For the given training corpus, find the optimal set of word sequences $\hat{\Gamma}$ using the algorithm in Figure 3.
2: Build the phrase sequence corpus from $\hat{\Gamma}$ acquired in step 1 by replacing the word sequence with its phrase.
3: For this phrase sequence corpus, find the optimal map $\hat{f}$ using the algorithm in Figure 2.

Figure 4: Combining the phrase and class methods.

4 Statistical Input Method based on a Phrase Class n-gram Model

In this section, we propose a method of combining the two language model improvements in the section 3 and construct a *phrase class n-gram model* so that we can realize the compact but accurate system. In addition, we also explain how to integrate the phrase class n-gram model into the statistical input method.

4.1 Combining the Phrase and Class Methods

A phrase model has less cross-entropy than a word model (Mori et al., 1997). Phrase modeling makes a more accurate language model. However the vocabulary size of phrase models is larger than that of word models, because some word sequences for phrases are added to the vocabulary of the phrase models. As a result, phrase models are often larger than word models.

This problem is solved by the method of class modeling. A class model is smaller than a word model (Brown et al., 1992; Kneser and Ney, 1993; Mori et al., 1998). A vocabulary size of a phrase model can be decreased by clustering the words and phrases in the vocabulary using the algorithm in Figure 2. Figure 4 shows our procedure of combining the two methods. As shown in this procedure, the clustering algorithm is applied to the phrase sequence corpus used for a phrase model.

4.2 Phrase Class n-gram Model

We can construct a phrase class n-gram model using a phrase sequence corpus and a function f that maps a phrase into its class. Because the phrase class n-gram model is made by combining the phrase and class methods, the mathematics of the phrase class n-gram model is also the combination of the mathematics of the two models.

Let $\boldsymbol{w} = w_1 w_2 \cdots w_m$ be an input sequence of words and f be a function that maps a phrase γ into its class c. In a phrase class model, like phrase models, $\boldsymbol{w}$ is converted to the phrase sequence $\boldsymbol{\gamma} = \gamma_1 \gamma_2 \cdots \gamma_{m'}$, which is corresponding to $\boldsymbol{w}$, and the phrase sequence $\boldsymbol{\gamma}$ is predicted.

$$
\begin{aligned}
p(\boldsymbol{w}) &\overset{def.}{=} p(\boldsymbol{\gamma}) \\
&= p(\gamma_1 \gamma_2 \cdots \gamma_{m'}) \\
&= \prod_{i=1}^{m'} p(\gamma_i | \gamma_1 \gamma_2 \cdots \gamma_{i-1}), \\
p(\gamma_i | \gamma_1 \gamma_2 \cdots \gamma_{i-1}) &\approx p(\gamma_i | \gamma_{i-k} \gamma_{i-k+1} \cdots \gamma_{i-1}).
\end{aligned}
$$

Then, like class models, the phrase class n-gram model predicts the i-th class referring to the last $k = n - 1$ classes and the i-th phrase referring to the i-th class.

$$p(\gamma_i|\gamma_{i-k}\gamma_{i-k+1}\cdots\gamma_{i-1}) \stackrel{def.}{=} p(c_i|c_{i-k}c_{i-k+1}\cdots c_{i-1})p(\gamma_i|c_i), \tag{4}$$

where $c_* = f(\gamma_*)$. $p(c_i|c_{i-k}c_{i-k+1}\cdots c_{i-1})$ and $p(\gamma_i|c_i)$ are defined by maximum likelihood from a training corpus.

$$p(c_i|c_{i-k}c_{i-k+1}\cdots c_{i-1}) \stackrel{def.}{=} \frac{N(c_{i-k}c_{i-k+1}\cdots c_{i-1}c_i)}{N(c_{i-k}c_{i-k+1}\cdots c_{i-1})}, \tag{5}$$

$$p(\gamma_i|c_i) \stackrel{def.}{=} \frac{N(\gamma_i)}{N(c_i)}. \tag{6}$$

The prediction unit of the phrase class n-gram model constructed here is a word. We can construct in the same way a phrase class n-gram model whose basic prediction unit is a word-pronunciation pair, and it can be applied to the input method in the section 2.2. In that case, γ_* in this section represents a word-pronunciation pair sequence.

4.3 Input Method based on a Phrase Class n-gram Model

We integrate the phrase class n-gram model, where the basic prediction unit is a word-pronunciation pair, and the unknown word model described in the section 2.5.

Given a pronunciation sequence $\boldsymbol{x}$ as an input, the goal of the input method is to output $\hat{\boldsymbol{w}}$ that maximizes the likelihood $p(\boldsymbol{w},\boldsymbol{x}) = p(\langle w_1,\boldsymbol{x}_1\rangle\langle w_2,\boldsymbol{x}_2\rangle\cdots\langle w_m,\boldsymbol{x}_m\rangle)$, as we explained in the section 2.2. We use a phrase class n-gram model whose basic prediction unit is a word-pronunciation pair to calculate $p(\langle w_1,\boldsymbol{x}_1\rangle\langle w_2,\boldsymbol{x}_2\rangle\cdots\langle w_m,\boldsymbol{x}_m\rangle)$. In the phrase class n-gram model, first $\langle w_1,\boldsymbol{x}_1\rangle\langle w_2,\boldsymbol{x}_2\rangle\cdots\langle w_m,\boldsymbol{x}_m\rangle$ is converted to the phrase sequence $\boldsymbol{\gamma} = \gamma_1\gamma_2\cdots\gamma_{m'}$, where the phrase γ_i represents a word-pronunciation pair sequence, and then $p(\boldsymbol{\gamma})$ is calculated as follows:

$$\begin{aligned} p(\langle w_1,\boldsymbol{x}_1\rangle\langle w_2,\boldsymbol{x}_2\rangle\cdots\langle w_m,\boldsymbol{x}_m\rangle) &\stackrel{def.}{=} p(\boldsymbol{\gamma}) \\ &= p(\gamma_1\gamma_2\cdots\gamma_{m'}) \\ &= \prod_{i=1}^{m'} p(\gamma_i|\gamma_1\gamma_2\cdots\gamma_{i-1}), \\ p(\gamma_i|\gamma_1\gamma_2\cdots\gamma_{i-1}) &\approx p(\gamma_i|\gamma_{i-k}\gamma_{i-k+1}\cdots\gamma_{i-1}). \end{aligned}$$

If γ_i is in the vocabulary of the phrase class n-gram model, by Equations (4), (5) and (6) we have

$$p(\gamma_i|\gamma_{i-k}\gamma_{i-k+1}\cdots\gamma_{i-1}) = \frac{N(c_{i-k}c_{i-k+1}\cdots c_{i-1}c_i)}{N(c_{i-k}c_{i-k+1}\cdots c_{i-1})}\frac{N(\gamma_i)}{N(c_i)}.$$

Otherwise, we approximate $p(\gamma_i|\gamma_{i-k}\gamma_{i-k+1}\cdots\gamma_{i-1})$ using the unknown word model $p(\boldsymbol{x})$ in the section 2.5 as follows:

$$p(\gamma_i|\gamma_{i-k}\gamma_{i-k+1}\cdots\gamma_{i-1}) \approx p(\boldsymbol{x}'_i),$$

where $\boldsymbol{x}'_i$ is the character sequence corresponding to γ_i.

usage	#sentences	#words	#chars
training	53,424	1,258,805	1,813,135
test	6,350	137,642	201,477

Table 1: Corpora.

5 Experiments

In order to test the effectiveness of combining the phrase and class methods, we constructed phrase class bi-gram using our method and compared the conversion accuracy and the model size of our model to other language models. In this section we show the experimental results and discuss them.

5.1 Experimental Settings

We used the core corpus of the Balanced Corpus of Contemporary Written Japanese (BCCWJ) (Maekawa, 2008) for the experiments. The BCCWJ is composed of two corpora, the BCCWJ-CORE corpus and the BCCWJ-NON-CORE corpus, and we used the BCCWJ-CORE. A sentence of the BCCWJ-CORE corpus is a sequence of pairs of a word and its pronunciation as shown in Figure 1. The word segmentation and pronunciation tagging were done manually.

We split the BCCWJ-CORE into two parts: one is for training language models and the other is for the test of them. Table 1 shows the specifications of the corpora.

We constructed language models and a vocabulary from the training corpus of the BCCWJ. The vocabulary was constructed according to (Mori et al., 1998) and (Mori et al., 1997).

The following is a list of language models we compared.

1. Word-pronunciation pair bi-gram model
2. Class bi-gram model (Prediction unit: Word-pronunciation pair)
3. Phrase bi-gram model
4. Phrase class bi-gram model (Prediction unit: Phrase)
5. Word-pronunciation pair tri-gram model

5.2 Criterions

One of the criterions we took in this paper is conversion accuracy. The conversion accuracy is measured by F measure, which is the harmonic mean of precision P and recall R. Let N_{CWJ} be the number of characters of a sentence in the BCCWJ for the test, N_{SYS} be the number of characters of a sentence that KKC outputs, and N_{LCS} be the number of characters of the longest common subsequence. The precision P is defined as N_{LCS}/N_{SYS} and the recall R is defined as N_{LCS}/N_{CWJ}. Hence F measure is $\frac{2}{1/P+1/R}$.

In addition to the conversion accuracy, we also evaluated our methods from the viewpoint of the size of language models. The size of a language model is measured by the vocabulary size and the number of non-zero frequency entries of bi-gram or tri-gram.

Model	Precision	Recall	F measure
Word-pronunciation pair bi-gram	89.86	90.32	90.09
Class bi-gram	89.78	90.28	90.03
Phrase bi-gram	90.26	90.53	90.39
Phrase class bi-gram	90.25	90.58	90.41
Word-pronunciation pair tri-gram	89.97	90.45	90.21

Table 2: Conversion accuracy

Model	Vocabulary size	#non-zero frequency entries
Word-pronunciation pair bi-gram	22,801	264,336
Class bi-gram	4,245	141,482
Phrase bi-gram	25,056	339,574
Phrase class bi-gram	5,550	206,978
Word-pronunciation pair tri-gram	22,801	645,996

Table 3: Model size

5.3 Results

Table 2 shows the conversion accuracies of the bi-gram models and the tri-gram model. Comparing the conversion accuracies of the word-pronunciation pair bi-gram model and the phrase bi-gram model, it can be said that phrase modeling makes better language models. Class modeling does not have a significant effect on the conversion accuracy by comparing the conversion accuracies of the word-pronunciation pair bi-gram model and the class bi-gram model. The phrase class model, which was constructed by our method, has the best F measure.

Table 3 shows the model sizes of the bi-gram models and the tri-gram model. The vocabulary size of the phrase bi-gram model is larger than that of the word-pronunciation pair bi-gram model. Generally, the vocabulary size of a phrase model is larger than that of a word model since the phrase model adds some phrases to its vocabulary. We see that word clustering or phrase clustering makes smaller language models. As the result of phrase clustering, the size of our phrase class bi-gram model is smaller than that of the word-pronunciation pair bi-gram model and the word-pronunciation pair tri-gram model.

5.4 Evaluation on Large Training Data

We performed another more practical experiment. In this experiment, we also constructed a phrase class bi-gram model and a word-pronunciation pair tri-gram model. We used the training corpus that has about 360,000 sentences mainly from BCCWJ-NON-CORE. The results are in table 4 and 5. We see that the phrase class bi-gram model is smaller and it has the comparable conversion accuracy as the word-pronunciation pair tri-gram model.

6 Conclusion

In this paper we proposed a method to improve the language model for KKC by combining the phrase and class methods. We used a word-pronunciation pair as the basic prediction unit of the language model and constructed a phrase class n-gram model. We compared the conversion accuracy and model size of the phrase class bi-gram model to the other models. The results showed that the phrase class bi-gram model is smaller and it has the comparable or better

Model	Precision	Recall	F measure
Phrase class bi-gram	91.38	91.80	91.59
Word-pronunciation pair tri-gram	91.23	91.80	91.51

Table 4: Conversion accuracy

Model	Vocabulary size	#non-zero frequency entries
Phrase class bi-gram	10,421	862,890
Word-pronunciation pair tri-gram	61,040	3,225,937

Table 5: Model size

conversion accuracy than that of the word-pronunciation pair tri-gram model. Therefore our method of combining the improvements of phrase and class modeling makes a smaller, more accurate language model for KKC.

Acknowledgments

This work was partially supported by Microsoft CORE 8 Project.

References

Brown, P. F., Pietra, V. J. D., deSouza, P. V., Lai, J. C., and Mercer, R. L. (1992). Class-based n-gram models of natural language. *Computational Linguistics*, 18(4):467–479.

Chen, Z. and Lee, K.-F. (2000). A new statistical approach to Chinese pinyin input. In *Proceedings of the 38th Annual Meeting of the Association for Computational Linguistics*, pages 241–247.

Deligne, S. and Bimbot, F. (1995). Language modeling by variable length sequences: Theoretical formulation and evaluation of multigrams. In *Proceedings of the International Conference on Acoustics, Speech, and Signal Processing*, pages 169–172.

Kneser, R. and Ney, H. (1993). Improved clustering techniques for class-based statistical language modelling. In *Proceedings of the Third European Conference on Speech Communication and Technology*, pages 973–976.

Maekawa, K. (2008). Balanced corpus of contemporary written Japanese. In *Proceedings of the 6th Workshop on Asian Language Resources*, pages 101–102.

Mori, S., Masatoshi, T., Yamaji, O., and Nagao, M. (1999). Kana-kanji conversion by a stochastic model. *Transactions of Information Processing Society of Japan*, 40(7):2946–2953. (in Japanese).

Mori, S., Nishimura, M., and Itoh, N. (1998). Word clustering for a word bi-gram model. In *Proceedings of the Fifth International Conference on Speech and Language Processing*.

Mori, S., Yamaji, O., and Nagao, M. (1997). An improvement of n-gram model by a change of the prediction unit. In *IPSJ SIG Technical Reports*, 97-SLP-19-14, pages 87–94. (In Japanese).

Ries, K., Buø, F. D., and Waibel, A. (1996). Class phrase models for language modeling. In *Proceedings of the Fourth International Conference on Speech and Language Processing*.

An Ensemble Model of Word-based and Character-based Models for Japanese and Chinese Input Method

Yoh OKUNO[1] *Shinsuke MORI*[2]
(1) SWIFTKEY, 91-95 Southwark Bridge Road, London, SE1 0AX, United Kingdom
(2) KYOTO UNIVERSITY, Yoshidahonmachi, Sakyo-ku, Kyoto, 606-8501, Japan
yoh@swiftkey.net, mori@ar.media.kyoto-u.ac.jp

Abstract

Since Japanese and Chinese languages have too many characters to be input directly using a standard keyboard, input methods for these languages that enable users to input the characters are required. Recently, input methods based on statistical models have become popular because of their accuracy and ease of maintenance. Most of them adopt word-based models because they utilize word-segmented corpora to train the models. However, such word-based models suffer from unknown words because they cannot convert words correctly which are not in corpora. To handle this problem, we propose a character-based model that enables input methods to convert unknown words by exploiting character-aligned corpora automatically generated by a monotonic alignment tool. In addition to the character-based model, we propose an ensemble model of both character-based and word-based models to achieve higher accuracy. The ensemble model combines these two models by linear interpolation. All of these models are based on joint source channel model to utilize rich context through higher order joint n-gram. Experiments on Japanese and Chinese datasets showed that the character-based model performs reasonably and the ensemble model outperforms the word-based baseline model. As a future work, the effectiveness of incorporating large raw data should be investigated.

KEYWORDS: Input Method, Machine Transliteration, Joint Source Channel Model, Automatic Alignment, Ensemble Method, Japanese, Chinese.

1 Introduction

There are more than 6,000 basic Kanji characters and 50 Hiragana/Katakana characters in Japanese language. A Kanji character represents one meaning, while Hiragana/Katakana characters represent their sounds. Therefore, it is difficult to input all kind of Japanese texts into computers or mobile phones by a standard keyboard which has only 100 keys. In order to input Japanese texts, it is common to use input methods called Kana-Kanji conversion, which convert Hiragana characters into Kanji or mixed characters. Since there are no spaces between words, most of Japanese input methods process texts sentence by sentence. Chinese language has nearly the same problem. There are more than 10,000 Hanzi characters in Chinese and Pinyin input methods are used to convert Roman characters into Chinese characters.

In these days, statistical models are used for such input methods to achieve high accuracy and automate parameter tuning (Mori et al., 1999; Chen and Lee, 2000). The statistical models are trained before actual conversion from corpora in each language. Sentences in these corpora are segmented word by word and annotated to specify the words' pronunciation, whether manually or automatically. Most of the models treat a word as an atomic unit; that means, they distinguish all words completely even if they share some characters in their strings. In this paper, we call such approaches *word-based* models.

However, such word-based models suffer from unknown words in principle, because they cannot convert or even enumerate a word in the candidate list when the word is not contained in the corpora. Instead of word-based models, we propose a new *character-based* model for input methods to avoid such a problem. In addition, we also propose an *ensemble model* which is a combination of both word-based and character-based models to achieve higher accuracy and take advantages of both models.

The rest of this paper is organized as follows: section 2 introduces related work, section 3 proposes the models, section 4 describes experimental results, and section 5 summarizes this paper and future work.

2 Related Work

There is a limited number of studies specialized in statistical models for input methods. However, closely related tasks such as machine transliteration, letter-to-phoneme conversion, language modeling, or machine translation share similar problems and solutions with input methods.

Early models for input methods adopt noisy channel model (Mori et al., 1999; Chen and Lee, 2000), which are less accurate than joint source channel model (Li et al., 2004). Conventionally, noisy channel model is used to divide joint model into conditional model and language model so that language model can be trained from large raw data such as crawled websites. Joint source channel model can also be combined such large raw data, though it is remained as a future work. In this paper, we focus on models for standard annotated corpora to keep the study reproducible and comparable with other works.

In noisy channel model, character n-gram is used as a back-off model for word n-gram model to address unknown word problem (Mori et al., 2006; Gao et al., 2002). However, character n-gram model does not exploit rich information of joint n-gram of word and its pronunciation. Moreover, it is not straightforward to extend character n-gram model to character-based joint n-gram model without recent development in alignment techniques we use (Jiampojamarn et al., 2007; Kubo et al., 2011).

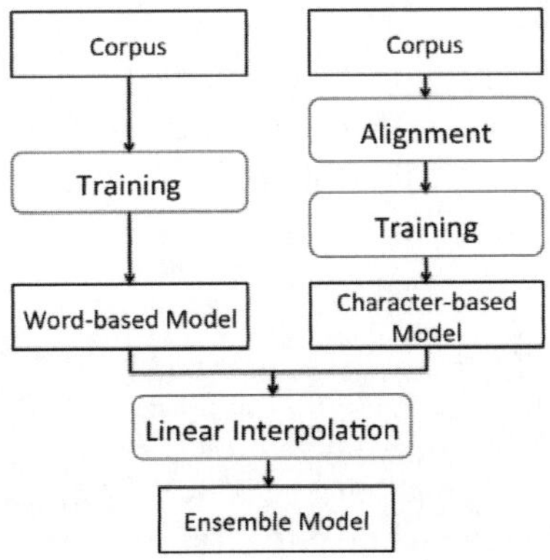

Figure 1: An Ensemble Model of Word-based and Character-based Models

Recently, discriminative models are introduced to input methods (Tokunaga et al., 2011; Jiampojamarn et al., 2008; Cherry and Suzuki, 2009), but they are impractical for higher order n-gram because of their large model size and long training time. Spelling correction is commonly incorporated with Chinese input methods (Zheng et al., 2011; Suzuki and Gao, 2012).

Machine transliteration is a similar task to input method, which translates proper names into foreign languages based on their sounds (Zhang et al., 2012). Machine transliteration is formulated as monotonic machine translation that is purely based on characters rather than words (Finch and Sumita, 2008). According to the manner of statistical machine translation (SMT), automatic alignment is applied to estimate character alignment between source and target strings (Jiampojamarn et al., 2007; Kubo et al., 2011).

Hatori and Suzuki (2011) solved Japanese pronunciation inference combining word-based and character-based features within SMT-style framework to handle unknown words. Neubig et al. (2012) proposed character-based SMT to incorporate word segmentation and handle sparsity. They solved different problems using similar solutions.

3 An Ensemble Model of Word-based and Character-based Models

We propose an ensemble model as a combination of word-based and character-based models. Figure 1 shows the training process for our model. The left side shows word-based model, while the right side shows character-based model. The difference between word-based model and character-based model is that later has an alignment step to produce character-aligned corpus by an automatic alignment tool. The two models are combined using linear interpolation to produce the final ensemble model.

Our model is built on top of joint source channel model (Li et al., 2004), which is an improvement on noisy channel model. In this section, we explain noisy channel model first, and joint source channel model next. Then the word-based model, the character-based model, and the ensemble model are explained.

3.1 Noisy Channel Model

A common statistical approach for input method is called noisy channel model, which models a conditional probability of output words given input strings to prioritize output candidates. The model decomposes the conditional distribution into language model and input model by Bayes rule:

$$P(Y|X) = \frac{P(Y)P(X|Y)}{P(X)} \propto P(Y)P(X|Y) \tag{1}$$

Y is the output sequence and X is the input sequence. Language model $P(Y)$ stands for how likely the output is in the language, while input model $P(X|Y)$ stands for how proper the pronunciation is.

A standard language model is n-gram model, which utilizes contexts of length $n-1$ to predict the current word y_i.

$$P(Y) = \prod_{i=1}^{L} P(y_i|y_{i-n+1}^{i-1}) \tag{2}$$

y_i is the i-th output word, x_i is corresponding input string, L is the length of output sequence, n is the order of n-gram model, and y_i^j is a output sequence from i to j.

Input model is usually simple unigram or uniform distribution assigned to possible pronunciations.

$$P(X|Y) = \prod_{i=1}^{L} P(x_i|y_i) \tag{3}$$

However, it has a problem to ignore context around the word, leading low accuracy in conversion.

3.2 Joint Source Channel Model

Joint source channel model (Li et al., 2004) adopts a joint distribution rather than conditional distribution;

$$P(Y|X) = \frac{P(X,Y)}{P(X)} \propto P(X,Y) \tag{4}$$

The joint distribution is modeled as joint n-gram sequence.

$$P(X,Y) = \prod_{i=1}^{L} P(x_i, y_i|x_{i-n+1}^{i-1}, y_{i-n+1}^{i-1}) \tag{5}$$

This enables exploiting rich context of joint distribution to achieve fine-grained joint model.

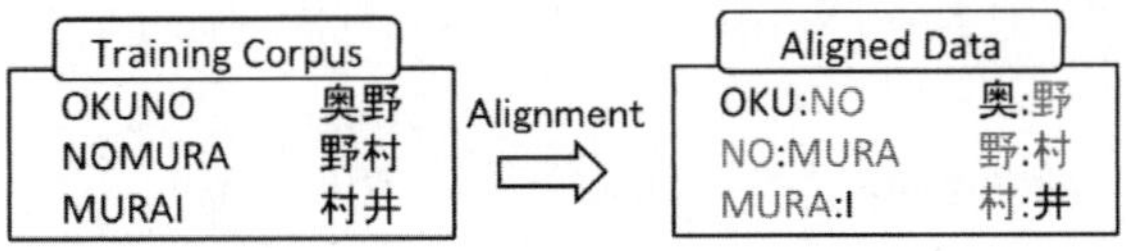

Figure 2: Alignment Step for Character-based Model

We adopt modified Kneser-Ney smoothing (Kneser and Ney, 1995) because it performed best in our experiment. *SRILM* (Stolcke, 2002) [1], which is a language model toolkit, is used for training n-gram models.

3.3 Word-based Model

In this study, we adopt the word-based model as a baseline model. The word-based model is trained from a word-segmented corpus. That means, the corpus is segmented word by word, and each word is annotated to specify its pronunciation. Each word and its pronunciation in the corpus are coupled into a unit to train a joint n-gram model.

This baseline model is strong enough if the corpus is properly segmented and annotated. It works well for words which are contained in the corpus. The ambiguity in homonyms are solved using their contexts through joint source channel model. However, the word-based model suffers from unknown words because it cannot properly handle words that are not in the corpus.

3.4 Character-based Model

In order to overcome the shortcomings of the word-based model, we propose a character-based model that is trained on character-aligned corpus. Since we do not have such a corpus, we need to produce a character-aligned corpus from a word-segmented corpus automatically. Though it is not trivial, recent development on character alignment tools enables it.

We adopted an alignment tool called *mpaligner* (Kubo et al., 2011) [2], which is suitable for this purpose. It assigns pronunciation to each character based on expectation maximization (EM) algorithm. Figure 2 shows how the alignment step works. Basically, it finds alignments between a character and its pronunciation based on co-occurrence in the corpus.

A word in the corpus is monotonically aligned one by one. That means, any words or pronunciations cannot be aligned across their word boundaries in the original corpus. Once the corpus is aligned, the training step is exactly same to the word-based model.

In addition to character alignment, mpaligner has a feature called many-to-many alignment that can find words whose pronunciations cannot be divided into combination of pronunciations for each character. This feature is effective especially in Japanese since Japanese language sometimes add its own pronunciation to Chinese words. For this reason, the result is not purely character-aligned, but most of characters are aligned to each pronunciation.

In Japanese and Chinese languages, it is common that a word contains only one character. Such a word is called a single character word. Most of words are consists of single character words and their pronunciations, while some words can not be represented as a combination of single character words because of its phonetic variation.

[1] http://www.speech.sri.com/projects/srilm/
[2] http://sourceforge.jp/projects/mpaligner/

Word	今日	大人	北京	一〇
Pronunciation	きょう	おとな	ぺきん	じゅう
Type	Combined	Combined	Combined	Combined

Word	日 本	自 分	情 報	関 係
Pronunciation	に ほん	じ ぶん	じょう ほう	かん けい
Type	Split	Split	Split	Split

Word	日 本	結 婚	三 菱	会 社
Pronunciation	にっ ぽん	けっ こん	みつ びし	がい しゃ
Type	Variation	Variation	Variation	Variation

Figure 3: Alignment Examples

Character alignment step reveals such phonetic variation of character which is not contained as a single character word. Pronunciation of a character can be changed when it is used in a word. When an unknown word contains such a pronunciation, the character-based model enables it to be converted correctly.

Figure 3 shows the examples of alignment result in Japanese. It shows pairs of word and its pronunciation with alignment type. Word and pronunciation are separated with spaces if the aligner split the word into characters. Each alignment type corresponds to features explained above; *combined* means that the word has unique pronunciation so it can not split into characters, *split* means that the word is split into characters and their pronunciations, and *variation* means that the word contains phonetic variation which does not appear in single character words.

3.5 Ensemble Model

Although the character-based model can capture unknown words, it achieves relatively poor compared to the word-based model in our experiment. There are two reasons why the character-based model does not work well. First, it tends to overfit to the training data because the corpus is segmented more finely. Second, the errors caused in the alignment step can be problematic.

In order to achieve higher accuracy, we propose an ensemble model which is linear interpolation of word-based model $P_w(X,Y)$ and character-based model $P_c(X,Y)$.

$$P(X,Y) = \alpha P_w(X,Y) + (1-\alpha)P_c(X,Y) \tag{6}$$

The interpolation weight α $(0 \leq \alpha \leq 1)$ means the ratio in which model is used. $\alpha = 1$ means pure word-based model, while $\alpha = 0$ means pure character-based model. $\alpha = 0.5$ is nearly equivalent to the model trained from corpora which is a concatenation of original corpus and character-aligned corpus.

α is determined empirically. In our experiment, α has an optimal value between 0.5 and 0.7. That means, both word-based and character based models are complementary to each other and the ratio of these two models should be a bit closer to word-based model.

Domain	Sentences	Data Source
OC	6,266	Yahoo! Q&A
OW	4,080	Government Document
OY	6,253	Yahoo! Blog
PN	11,582	Newspaper
PB	6,645	Book
PM	9,356	Magazine
ALL	44,182	All of above

Table 1: Details of BCCWJ

4 Experiment

To confirm the effectiveness and properties of our models, we conducted experiments on Japanese and Chinese corpora in various situations. We divided each corpus into 90% of training data and 10% of test data, trained our models and evaluated on test data. The models are evaluated by comparing system output and gold standard; system output is produced by a decoder which is an implementation of Viterbi algorithm for higher order n-gram models [3].

4.1 Data Set

For Japanese corpus, we adopt BCCWJ (Balanced Corpus of Contemporary Written Japanese) (Maekawa, 2008). BCCWJ is a corpus in various domains. It is annotated both by human and machine learning algorithm. We use human-annotated part which consists of 44,182 sentences. Table 1 shows the details.

For Chinese corpus, we adopt LCMC (The Lancaster Corpus of Mandarin Chinese) (McEnery et al., 2003). It has Hanzi and Pinyin pairs, but the Pinyin part of the corpus is annotated automatically. It contains 45,595 lines from 15 domains.

4.2 Evaluation Metric

We adopt evaluation metrics based on the longest common sequence (LCS) between system output and gold standard following (Mori et al., 1999) and (Tokunaga et al., 2011).

$$precision = \frac{N_{LCS}}{N_{SYS}} \tag{7}$$

$$recall = \frac{N_{LCS}}{N_{DAT}} \tag{8}$$

$$F\text{-}score = 2\frac{precision \cdot recall}{precision + recall} \tag{9}$$

Here, N_{LCS} is the length of the LCS, N_{SYS} is the length of the system output sequence, N_{DAT} is the length of gold standard. Note that LCS is not necessarily a continuous string contained in both string; that means, LCS can be concatenation of separated strings which are contained in both strings in order. CER (Character Error Rate) and ACC (Sentence Accuracy) are also shown for convenience, but F-score is used as our main metric.

[3]https://github.com/nokuno/jsc

Model	N	Precision	Recall	F-score	CER	ACC	Size
Word	2	0.932	0.932	0.932	0.088	0.334	4.3MB
Char	4	0.925	0.922	0.923	0.099	0.292	3.1MB
Ensemble	3	0.937	0.936	0.937	0.082	0.349	8.7MB

Table 2: Result for Japanese

Model	N	Precision	Recall	F-score	CER	ACC	Size
Word	2	0.958	0.958	0.958	0.044	0.505	4.6MB
Char	4	0.950	0.950	0.950	0.053	0.428	3.3MB
Ensemble	3	0.958	0.958	0.958	0.045	0.496	8.8MB

Table 3: Result for Chinese with tone

Model	N	Precision	Recall	F-score	CER	ACC	Size
Word	3	0.895	0.895	0.895	0.109	0.297	5.1MB
Char	3	0.871	0.871	0.871	0.133	0.210	3.3MB
Ensemble	4	0.895	0.895	0.895	0.111	0.274	8.7MB

Table 4: Result for Chinese without tone

4.3 Result Summary

Table 2, Table 3, Table 4 show the summary of our experiments to compare three models; word-based, character-based and ensemble models. The value of n is chosen to perform the best in terms of F-score.

In Japanese language, the word-based model outperforms the character-based model, and the ensemble model outperforms the word-based model consistently in all metrics.

In LCMC corpus, we could not find any improvement in the ensemble model over the word-based model. This is reasonable because the corpus is automatically annotated word by word. In our experiment, we found tone (1-4 digits) information reduces the ambiguity of pinyin input method greatly. Rest of experiments are conducted on Japanese corpus.

Model size and decoding time depend on the implementation of decoder which is not focus in this study, but we showed file size for each model in SRILM binary format. We can see that character-based model is smaller than word-based model whereas ensemble model is bigger than word-based model.

4.4 N-gram Order

Figure 4 shows F-score for three models with various n values from 1 to 10. It is notable that the character-based model performs best when $n = 4$ or larger, while $n = 2$ is enough for the word-based model. This shows that the character-based model requires longer context than the word-based model because it splits words into shorter characters. The ensemble model performs best when $n = 3$ which is middle of word-based and character-based models. In all models, higher order than the best order did not degrade the performance under the modified Kneser-Ney smoothing.

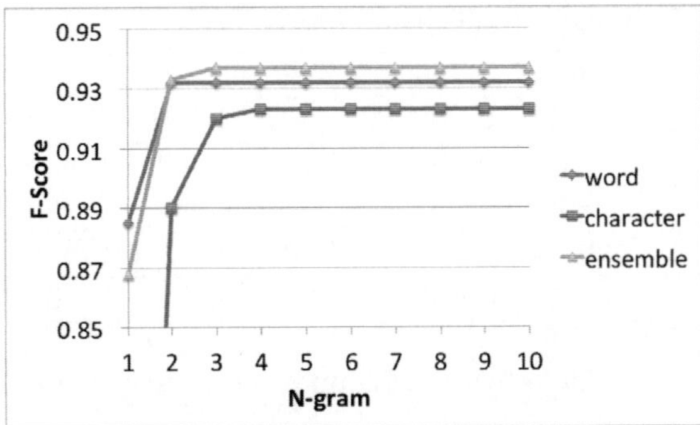

Figure 4: N-gram Order

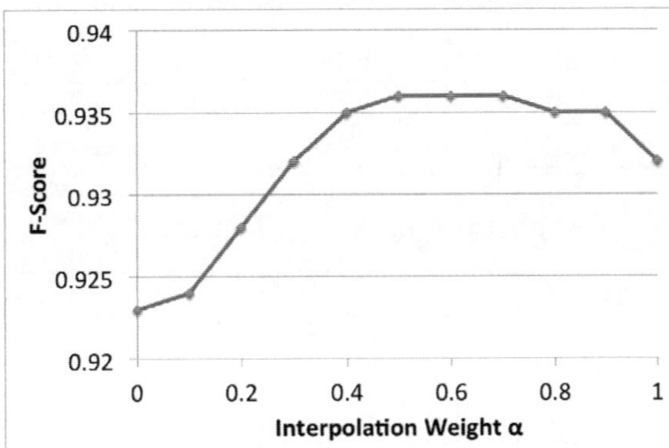

Figure 5: Interpolation Weight

4.5 Interpolation Weight

To investigate the effect of interpolation weight, we changed α from 0 (pure character-based) to 1 (pure word-based) by interval of 0.1. The result in Figure 5 shows that the weight from 0.5 to 0.7 is optimal in this case. That means, the two models are complementary to each other and the word-based model can be ameliorated by mixing the character-based model.

4.6 Cross Domain Analysis

In practice, it is important to choose right domain for training corpus. Table 5 shows F-score when the categories in training corpus and test corpus are different. To compare domains fairly, the smallest size of corpus is adopted; that means, we used only 4,080 sentences from each corpus. Therefore, the absolute F-score is relatively low. As we expected, the accuracy is the highest when the domain of training and testing corpus is the same. In addition, we can see that clean corpora such as newspaper or magazines can outperform corpus from web. It is possible to combine large general corpus and small but specific corpus to achieve more higher accuracy.

4.7 Smoothing Methods

Table 6 shows F-score of different smoothing methods. In our experiment, modified Kneser-Ney smoothing performed better than other smoothing methods.

Train | Test	OC	OW	OY	PB	PM	PN
OC	0.869	0.744	0.774	0.779	0.750	0.705
OW	0.749	0.966	0.701	0.759	0.717	0.747
OY	0.822	0.782	0.846	0.791	0.755	0.746
PB	0.807	0.761	0.755	0.902	0.754	0.740
PM	0.837	0.811	0.794	0.828	0.876	0.764
PN	0.812	0.848	0.762	0.820	0.783	0.867

Table 5: Cross Domain Analysis

Smoothing	Precision	Recall	F-score	CER	ACC
Modified Kneser-Ney	0.931	0.932	0.931	0.087	0.361
Witten-Bell	0.929	0.930	0.930	0.090	0.338
Absolute discounting	0.929	0.931	0.930	0.090	0.343
Ristad's natural discounting law	0.925	0.927	0.926	0.094	0.322
Add one smoothing	0.798	0.819	0.808	0.223	0.174

Table 6: Smoothing Methods

Pruning Threshold	F-score	1-gram size	2-gram size	3-gram size	File size
1e-4	0.808	345416	2232	144	15MB
1e-5	0.877	345416	27450	3345	15MB
1e-6	0.914	345416	222883	72087	17MB
1e-7	0.936	345416	1200021	833593	34MB
1e-8	0.942	345416	5286912	4146260	98MB

Table 7: Pruning Effect

4.8 Pruning Effect

In practical input methods, model size is important because the memory in a device is limited. In order to reduce model size, we applied entropy pruning (Stolcke, 2000) to word-based model. Table 7 shows the result of F-score, N-gram size and file size in the SRILM binary format for various thresholds. In this experiment, all data in BCCWJ including automatically annotated one is used to confirm the effectiveness of big data. The result shows practical tradeoff between model size and accuracy; more larger model might improve accuracy in the future.

4.9 Error Analysis

Figure 6 shows some examples of output from the ensemble model and the word-based model, and correct output. There are some typical cases where the ensemble model outperforms the word-based model: 1) casual expression, 2) foreign words, 3) number expression.

Last four lines show the samples where the ensemble model did not work well. In these examples, the character-based model breaks the correct result. From these analysis, we can see the effectiveness of our ensemble model not only in unknown words, but also sparseness of training corpus. In most cases, the ensemble model showed consistent results in one sentence while the word-based model break the consistency because of its sparseness.

Type	Sentence
Ensemble	プレイしまいまま引退しそうって話です。
Word	プレイ姉妹ママ引退しそうって話です。
Ensemble	騙されたと思ってやってみてちょ＾＾
Word	騙されたと思ってやってみて著＾＾
Ensemble	レオナルド・ディカプリオ。
Word	レオなるド・ディかぶ理生。
Ensemble	パーカッションミュージアム
Word	パー買っ所ん見ゅー時ア無
Ensemble	利用率は７３．２％
Word	利用率は七十三・２％
Ensemble	メールモダメ。
Correct	メールもダメ。
Ensemble	ハリウッてもらったら、
Correct	針打ってもらったら、

Figure 6: Error Analysis

Conclusion

In this paper, we proposed an ensemble model of word-based and character-based models. The character-based model exploit a character alignment tool to aquire fine-grained model. The expriments showed that the ensemble model outperforms the word-based model and character-based model performs modestly. The optimal n for the character-based model and the ensemble model was longer than word-based model. The optimal interpolation weight for ensemble model was 0.5 to 0.7, which is close to the word-based model. As a future work, the effectiveness of unannotated corpora such as crawled web pages should be confirmed. In practice, it is important to integrate various corpora into single model. It is possible to apply discriminative models to character-based model or ensemble model if we can train and decode the model for higher order n-gram features effectively.

References

Chen, Z. and Lee, K.-F. (2000). A new statistical approach to chinese pinyin input. In *Proceedings of the 38th Annual Meeting of the Association for Computational Linguistics*, pages 241–247, Hong Kong. Association for Computational Linguistics.

Cherry, C. and Suzuki, H. (2009). Discriminative substring decoding for transliteration. In *Proceedings of the 2009 Conference on Empirical Methods in Natural Language Processing*, pages 1066–1075, Singapore. Association for Computational Linguistics.

Finch, A. and Sumita, E. (2008). Phrase-based machine transliteration. In *Proceedings of the Workshop on Technologies and Corpora for Asia-Pacific Speech Translation (TCAST)*, pages 13–18, Hyderabad, India.

Gao, J., Goodman, J., Li, M., and Lee, K.-F. (2002). Toward a unified approach to statistical language modeling for chinese. 1(1):3–33.

Hatori, J. and Suzuki, H. (2011). Japanese pronunciation prediction as phrasal statistical machine translation. In *Proceedings of 5th International Joint Conference on Natural Language Processing*, pages 120–128, Chiang Mai, Thailand. Asian Federation of Natural Language Processing.

Jiampojamarn, S., Cherry, C., and Kondrak, G. (2008). Joint processing and discriminative training for letter-to-phoneme conversion. In *Proceedings of ACL-08: HLT*, pages 905–913, Columbus, Ohio. Association for Computational Linguistics.

Jiampojamarn, S., Kondrak, G., and Sherif, T. (2007). Applying many-to-many alignments and hidden markov models to letter-to-phoneme conversion. In *Human Language Technologies 2007: The Conference of the North American Chapter of the Association for Computational Linguistics; Proceedings of the Main Conference*, pages 372–379, Rochester, New York. Association for Computational Linguistics.

Kneser, R. and Ney, H. (1995). Improved backing-off for m-gram language modeling. In *Acoustics, Speech, and Signal Processing, 1995. ICASSP-95., 1995 International Conference on*, volume 1, pages 181–184. IEEE.

Kubo, K., Kawanami, H., Saruwatari, H., and Shikano, K. (2011). Unconstrained many-to-many alignment for automatic pronunciation annotation. In *Proceedings of Asia-Pacific Signal and Information Processing Association Annual Summit and Conference 2011 (APSIPA2011)*, Xi'an, China.

Li, H., Zhang, M., and Su, J. (2004). A joint source-channel model for machine transliteration. In *Proceedings of the 42nd Meeting of the Association for Computational Linguistics (ACL'04), Main Volume*, pages 159–166, Barcelona, Spain.

Maekawa, K. (2008). Balanced corpus of contemporary written japanese. In *Proceedings of the 6th Workshop on Asian Language Resources*, pages 101–102.

McEnery, A., Xiao, Z., and Mo, L. (2003). Aspect marking in english and chinese: using the lancaster corpus of mandarin chinese for contrastive language study. *Literary and Linguistic Computing*, 18(4):361–378.

Mori, S., Masatoshi, T., Yamaji, O., and Nagao, M. (1999). Kana-kanji conversion by a stochastic model (in japanese). *Transactions of IPSJ*, 40(7):2946–2953.

Mori, S., Takuma, D., and Kurata, G. (2006). Phoneme-to-text transcription system with an infinite vocabulary. In *Proceedings of the 21st International Conference on Computational Linguistics and the 44th annual meeting of the Association for Computational Linguistics*, ACL-44, pages 729–736, Stroudsburg, PA, USA. Association for Computational Linguistics.

Neubig, G., Watanabe, T., Mori, S., and Kawahara, T. (2012). Machine translation without words through substring alignment. In *The 50th Annual Meeting of the Association for Computational Linguistics (ACL)*, pages 165–174, Jeju, Korea.

Stolcke, A. (2000). Entropy-based pruning of backoff language models. *arXiv preprint cs/0006025*.

Stolcke, A. (2002). Srilm-an extensible language modeling toolkit. In *Seventh International Conference on Spoken Language Processing*.

Suzuki, H. and Gao, J. (2012). A unified approach to transliteration-based text input with online spelling correction. In *Proceedings of the 2012 Joint Conference on Empirical Methods in Natural Language Processing and Computational Natural Language Learning*, pages 609–618, Jeju Island, Korea. Association for Computational Linguistics.

Tokunaga, H., Okanohara, D., and Mori, S. (2011). Discriminative method for japanese kana-kanji input method. In *Proceedings of the Workshop on Advances in Text Input Methods (WTIM 2011)*, pages 10–18, Chiang Mai, Thailand. Asian Federation of Natural Language Processing.

Zhang, M., Kumaran, A., and Li, H. (2012). Whitepaper of news 2012 shared task on machine transliteration. In *Proceedings of the 4th Named Entities Workshop (NEWS 2012)*, Jeju, Korea. The Association of Computational Linguistics.

Zheng, Y., Li, C., and Sun, M. (2011). Chime: An efficient error-tolerant chinese pinyin input method. In *Proceedings of the 22nd International Joint Conference on Artificial Intelligence*.

Multi-objective Optimization for Efficient Brahmic Keyboards

Albert Brouillette[1] *Dr. Utpal Sharma*[2]
Dr. Jugal Kalita[1]
(1) University of Colorado, Colorado Springs, Colorado, USA
(2) Tezpur University, Napaam, Assam, India
abrouil2@uccs.edu, utpal@tezu.ernet.in, jkalita@uccs.edu

ABSTRACT
The development of efficient keyboards is an important element of effective human-computer interaction. This paper explores the use of multi-objective optimization and machine learning to create more effective keyboards. While previous research has focused on simply improving the expected typing speed of keyboards, this research utilizes multiple optimization criteria to create a more robust keyboard configuration. As these criteria are incorporated, they will often conflict with each other making this a complex optimization problem. Machine learning techniques were utilized and were proven to be an effective tool in keyboard optimization. The results reported here demonstrate that multi-objective genetic algorithms can be used to efficiently generate optimized keyboards. An English keyboard designed after 20000 generations was able to double the efficiency of the unoptimized QWERTY keyboard for multiple constraints. Despite having twice the number of characters, an Assamese keyboard was generated that performed better than the QWERTY layout.

KEYWORDS: Soft keyboards, user interfaces, Brahmic scripts, optimization, genetic algorithms, Android development..

1 Introduction

As technology progresses, it is important that user interfaces improve the efficiency of information transfer between users and computers. Because keyboards are a continuing, integral part of human-computer interactions, research into improving their efficiency is particularly valuable to improving data entry. The speed at which a user can input data can be greatly affected by the arrangement of keys on a keyboard. Based on the large number of possible key combinations, hand optimizing a keyboard is a tedious process. The use of artificial intelligence can make the process of generating optimal user interfaces much more efficient.

There are multiple considerations in determining the effectiveness of a keyboard. For example, the size, position and spacing of the keys on the device being used can dramatically change the speed that a user can input data. Additional factors such as accommodating user disability and adjusting to user preference can also affect the usability of a keyboard. An effective keyboard needs to be adaptable to the specific needs of each user. Touch-screen devices, with their soft-keyboards, have the potential to provide the flexibility required to adapt to these constraints. Since all of these factors are interconnected, it is difficult to accurately model them separately.

Previous research projects have used single objective optimization to increase the typing speed of a keyboard. While this method has produced good results, it ignores other factors that affect efficient typing. These machine generated keyboards could be more useful if a broader selection of constraints is used. This more generalized approach would allow optimization based on a wide variety of constraints such as ease of learning or user disability. The result of the optimization process is a set of optimal solutions that consider all of the constraints with a variety of weights.

This paper discusses the use of multi-objective optimization in creating efficient keyboards. In order to demonstrate value of this research on a global scale, we chose to develop keyboards for two very different languages, English and Assamese. Assamese is an Indic language from Northeast India, spoken by about thirty million people. The number of characters in this language makes the problem more complex and allows us to develop a more generic approach to the solution. We use Assamese as an exemplar of languages of the Indic class of languages, which are spoken by a more than a billion people, particularly in South Asia. At this time, these languages suffer from a lack of efficient and easily learned soft keyboards

The first constraint to consider is the typing speed, based on the expected typing style of the user. For example, some users will use a single finger, while others might use both of their thumbs for input. Another constraint for consideration is the ease with which a user can learn the layout of the keyboard. This can be represented as a constraint where the keyboard is biased toward a familiar, existing layout.

As constraints are added, some of them may conflict with each other, requiring a compromise to be made. The use of multi-objective genetic algorithms has been an effective and efficient approach to solving complex optimization problems(Konak et al., 2006). Multi-objective genetic algorithms allow the solutions to be optimized based on all of the objectives simultaneously. A solution is considered optimal if it performs better than or equal to the other solutions for every constraint. These optimal solutions will form a set known as a pareto front (Figure 1). This front contains the most efficient solutions, each involving a different compromise between the objectives. The set of solutions can be saved and accessed by the user based on their individual needs.

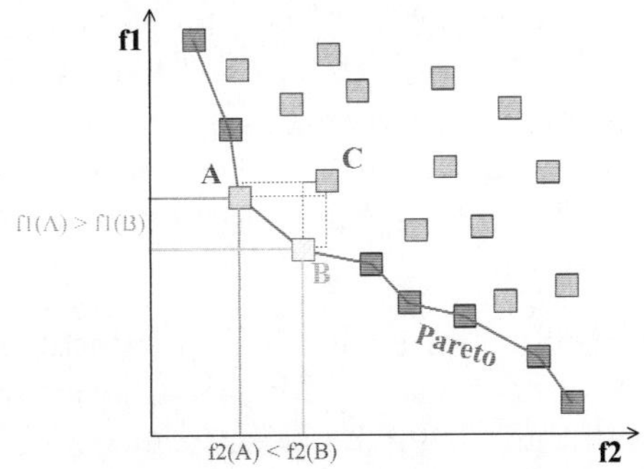

Figure 1: A simplified example of a pareto frontier. The darker points are the set of pareto optimal solutions. Source: WIKIPEDIA

2 Related Research

Some of the earliest research in modeling human-computer interaction was done by Fitts in the 1950's(Fitts, 1954). The model developed was able to compute the average time required for a human to move between two targets. Fitts' model is commonly expressed as the equation:

$$MT = \frac{1}{IP} \log_2 \left(\frac{D}{W} + 1 \right) \tag{1}$$

where IP is the index of performance for the device, D is the distance between the targets, and W is the size of the target.

This model has been used by many other researchers to estimate the time required for a human to move between controls in a graphical user interface(MacKenzie, 1992).

MacKenzie extended Fitts' law to model the human input speed on with a QWERTY keyboard on a mobile device(MacKenzie and Soukoreff, 2002). This model was later compared with human testing data and was shown to be a reasonably accurate estimate of actual human performance(Clarkson et al.).

In addition to analyzing the physical action of pressing the keys on the keyboard, researchers have also investigated the ability of users to learn a new keyboard layout. As researchers have worked on optimizing keyboards, it has been acknowledged that one of the limiting factors in users typing speed is the time spent searching for the keys(MacKenzie and Zhang, 1999). Smith and Zhai suggested adding an alphabetic bias to an optimized keyboard(Smith and Zhai, 2001). Lee and Zhai investigated techniques to help users quickly learn a new keyboard(P. U. Lee, 2004).

Much of the early development in keyboard design focused on creating variations of alphabetic and QWERTY layouts for the English language. The primary objective was to improve the ability of the keyboard to conform to mechanical limitations.

As technology improved, designers were able to focus on improving the typing speed of the keyboards. MacKenzie created one of the first character-frequency optimized layouts, the OPTI keyboard(MacKenzie and Zhang, 1999). The use of the Metropolis random walk algorithm was able to further increase the efficiency of soft keyboards(Zhai et al., 2000). These techniques have been able to improve expected typing speed up to 42 WPM.

Genetic algorithms have been used to achieve even higher levels of efficiency in keyboard design(Raynal and Vigouroux, 2005). (Hinkle et al., 2010) and (Hinkle et al., 2012) had worked extensively with optimization of Assamese and other Indic language keyboards. Their optimization was carried out with the single objective of maximization of input speed. They had created four different soft keyboards for Assamese: flat alphabetic, layered alphabetic, flat GA-designed and layered GA-designed.[1]

Gajos and Weld developed a technique for evaluating the effectiveness of user interfaces with respect to the individual needs of each user. With this analysis, they were able to generate personalized user interfaces with their SUPPLE project(Gajos et al., 2010).

3 Genetic Algorithm Optimization

The multi-objective optimization for this project was done using the NSGA-II multi-objective genetic algorithm(Deb et al., 2002). This algorithm was chosen based on its efficiency and effectiveness in multi-objective optimization. The algorithm was implemented using the JCLEC Java library[2]. This is an open-source library that provides implementations for several genetic algorithms.

For the purpose of keyboard design, two evaluators were written for designing keyboards on two devices. One evaluates the keyboard for its effectiveness for use as an on-screen keyboard for a desktop computer accessed with a mouse. The other evaluator tests the keyboard's effectiveness for both single finger and two-thumb input on a touch-screen mobile phone. The genetic algorithm was implemented using ordered crossover for recombination. As in (Hinkle et al., 2012), a mutation probability of 0.08% was used.

3.1 Preparation and General Keyboard Layout

Before starting the optimization process, it was necessary to determine a basic shape and pattern for the keyboards. In his research on user interface design, Ahlström found that expert users can make selections 35% faster from a square menu(Ahlström et al., 2010). Hinkle used a square layout for designing keyboards for Brahmic scripts (Hinkle et al., 2012). Based on this research, we decided that the on-screen keyboards should be designed assuming an essentially square shape with the keys being filled starting at the top.

This approach was impractical for a mobile device because the necessary size of the keyboard would have filled the entire screen. A practical solution to this problem was to base the keyboards on a variation of the QWERTY keyboard commonly used on mobile devices. Understandably, this shape would not work for languages with more characters. We designed the keyboards for the Assamese language assuming the use of two smaller QWERTY-shaped keyboards. The user can quickly switch between these keyboards as they type.

The first experiment was to establish a basis for comparison by evaluating the unoptimized QWERTY layout with the fitness function. The result was an estimated typing speed of 47 WPM for the first objective. The second objective reported on average distance of 2.88 keys between two characters in the same group. This analysis is shown in Figure 2.

[1]The first two were created by hand and the last two were created by single-objective GA optimization. The first was simply an alphabetic layout of the keys on a single keyboard and the second had a layer of alphabetic diacritics that popped up when one typed a consonant. The third was similar to the first, and the fourth to the second. The assumption in all four of these keyboards was that one types with a single finger. In addition, there was only one board

Figure 2: The analysis of the QWERTY keyboard using our evaluator. This layout has an estimated typing speed of 47 WPM and an average distance of 2.88 keys between two characters in the same group. The lower diagram shows the group number of each character.

3.2 Values for Fitts' Law Constants

Our evaluation of the keyboards relies on Fitts' Law to estimate the top typing speed for each keyboard layout. In order to accurately calculate the input speed for each device, it was first necessary to measure the Fitts' law Index of Performance(IP) for each device. This requires human testing to find the average movement time on each device. The approach to this calculation is similar to that used by Zhai(Zhai, 2004). For this experiment, we gave the human testers a series of randomly placed targets of varying sizes. The average time between targets was measured and used to calculate the Index of Performance based on the Index of Difficulty(ID).

3.2.1 Setting up the Experiment

The equation to calculate the IP for Fitts' Law is:

$$IP = \frac{ID}{MT} \tag{2}$$

where

$$ID = \log_2\left(\frac{D}{W} + 1\right) \tag{3}$$

The basic approach to this calculation is to have a user move between two targets with a varying ID with the test program calculating the average time(MT) between the targets. After several tests, it is possible to use the average ID and MT to calculate the IP for the current device. A program was used to generate random targets and calculate the time required to move between them(See Figure 3).

in each case. We present a comparison of these keyboards with our results in Table 3 .

[2]Available at http://jclec.sourceforge.net/

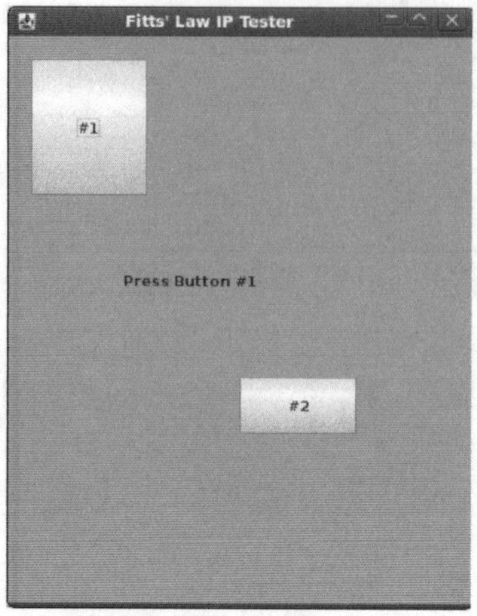

Figure 3: A screenshot of the IP testing program.

	Average Time	Average ID	IP
Mouse	0.53	2.58	4.9
Touch-screen: Right thumb	0.54	2.58	4.8
Touch-screen: Left thumb	0.63	2.58	4.1

Table 1: Results of IP test.

3.2.2 Results

The test program was used to calculate the IP for two applications. The results were obtained from 1000 data points after 100 consistent calculations. The first device was a desktop computer accessed using a mouse. This returned an IP value of 4.9. The second test was with a touch-screen device. The goal of this test was to calculate the constants for two-thumb typing. This required a separate calculation for each thumb. The result for a right-handed user was an IP of 4.8 for the right thumb and an IP of 4.1 for the left thumb.

3.3 Objective Constraints: Typing Speed

A primary objective in the keyboard optimization problem is to increase the typing speed. Our approach is to reduce the average time needed to move between two characters. This should result in the highest frequency characters being placed close together, minimizing the movement distance.

The average time between characters is calculated using an adaptation of Fitts' Law.

$$\bar{t} = \sum_{i=1}^{n}\sum_{j=1}^{n} \frac{P_{ij}}{IP}\left[\log_2\left(\frac{D_{ij}}{W_i}+1\right)\right] \tag{4}$$

where P_{ij} is the frequency of each digraph, IP is the calculated Index of Performance for the current device, D_{ij} is the distance between the two keys, and W_i is the width of each key. When a digraph consists of a repeated letter, it is assumed to take constant time. The experimental value for this constant is 0.127.

For two-thumb typing on the touch screen device, we calculate the average time between characters using a method similar to MacKenzie's model(MacKenzie and Soukoreff, 2002). The Fitt's law equation is used when the digraph is formed from two characters pressed with the same thumb. When the digraph consists of characters pressed with opposite thumbs, the mean time is chosen to be the greatest value between, either $^1/_2$ of the constant T_{REPEAT}, or the Fitts' law calculation to move from the character last pressed by that thumb. For the Assamese two-keyboard arrangement, we add an experimental constant value for the average time required to change between keyboards.

3.4 Objective Constraints: Ease of Learning

The simplest approach to creating an easy to learn interface is follow a pattern that is already familiar to the users. Smith and Zhai did research comparing the performance of novice users on optimized keyboards with and without an alphabetic bias(Smith and Zhai, 2001). Given two keyboards with similar predicted typing speeds, they found that the users were able to learn the alphabetic biased keyboard more quickly and performed up to 10% better.

The approach taken in this paper is to group alphabetically close characters together. For each language, we organized the characters into groups based on their position in the alphabet.

We implemented this constraint as a minimization problem for the average distance between any two characters in the same group. It should be noted that this does not consider the time between characters, it is simply the visual distance between the characters. The objective is to allow the user to more quickly find each character in these smaller alphabetic clusters.

3.5 Groups Split Across Two Keyboards

This constraint is an extension to the ease of learning that is unique to the Assamese mobile keyboard. The layout of the Assamese mobile keyboard is split between two smaller, QWERTY-sized keyboards. This constraint prevents the character groups from being split between the two keyboards. This is implemented as a penalty for keyboards that have many split groups. The goal is to minimize the number of split groups.

4 English Keyboard Optimization

We used the English language as our basis for comparison with the other languages. The smaller character set made it easier to evaluate the results of the optimization.

The specific keyboard shape for the single-input on-screen keyboard, was a 6×5 square grid. The two-input mobile keyboard was modeled after the QWERTY layout. For the ease of learning constraint, we created 5 character groups, {{a, b, c, d, e, f},{g, h, i...}...}.

4.1 Optimization: Single-Input

Using the specifications above, we used the genetic algorithm to optimize the key positions. The optimized keyboard was generated from a population of 5000 solutions allowed to evolve over 20000 generations. The result was a pareto front containing 900 optimal solutions. For a representative solution, we selected the solution with the highest ratio (Objective 1/Objective

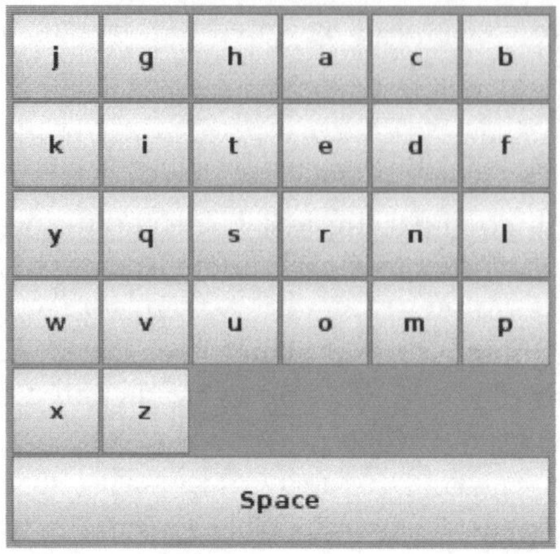

Figure 4: Optimized English keyboard generated with a population of 5000 over 20000 generations. This layout has an estimated typing speed of 46 WPM and an average distance of 1.1 keys between two characters in the same group.

2). The evaluator reported this solution as having an estimated typing speed of 46.43 WPM and an average distance of 1.1 keys between two characters in the same group(See Figure 4).

4.2 Optimization: Two-Input Mobile Keyboard

We ran a test with a population of 5000 solutions evaluated over 20000 generations. This experiment generated a large set of optimal keyboard layouts. A representative solution had an estimated typing speed of 84.2 WPM and an average distance of 1.43 keys between two characters in the same group(See Figure 5). Based on the evaluator, this keyboard performs nearly 2 times well as the QWERTY keyboard for both of the constraints.

4.3 Optimization: Three-Constraint Mobile Keyboard

In order to observe how a compromise is made between a set of constraints, we wanted to run the genetic algorithm with more constraints. For a final test we set up the algorithm to optimize a mobile keyboard for both single finger and two-thumb input. The goal of this experiment was to create a more universal keyboard that would allow a user to typing with either of these techniques. We maintained the ease of learning constraint so this test implemented three constraints.

This keyboard was designed based on the QWERTY shape like the two-input mobile keyboard. In Figure 6, we show a representative keyboard from the pareto set. This keyboard has an estimated typing speed of 81.99 WPM for two-thumb input and 26.96 WPM for single-finger input. There is an average distance of 1.46 keys between two characters from the same group.

4.4 Human Testing

The human testing had two objectives: to prove that this keyboard was an improvement over an unoptimized alphabetic layout and to show that our ease of learning constraint was effective in improving typing rates for novice users.

The human testers were given two different keyboards selected from the pareto front: the

Figure 5: Optimized English mobile keyboard generated with a population of 5000 over 20000 generations. This layout has an estimated typing speed of 84 WPM and an average distance of 1.43 keys between two characters in the same group. The lower diagram shows the group number of each character.

Figure 6: English keyboard optimized for both single finger and two-thumb input. This keyboard was generated with a population of 5000 over 20000 generations. This layout has an estimated typing speed of 82 WPM for two-thumb input and 27 WPM for single-finger input. There is an average distance of 1.46 keys between two characters in the same group. The lower diagram shows the group number of each character.

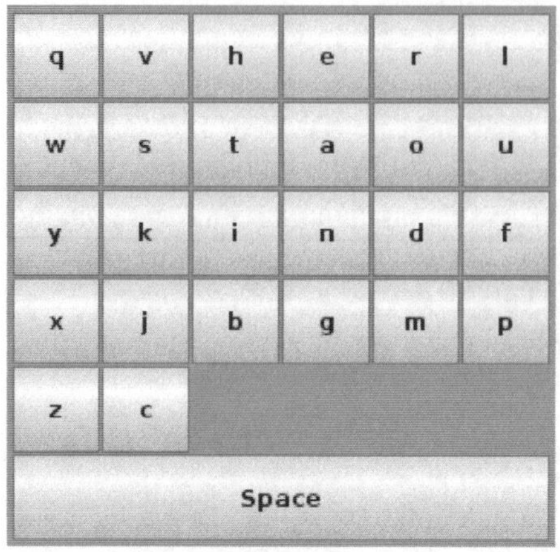

Figure 7: Optimized English keyboard generated with a population of 5000 over 20000 generations. This layout has an estimated typing speed of 50 WPM and an average distance of 1.9 keys between two characters in the same group.

keyboard with the highest predicted typing speed(See Figure 7), and the keyboard with the best compromise between the two objectives(Shown above in Figure 4). In order to facilitate a reasonable comparison, the testing process was similar to that used by Smith and Zhai(Smith and Zhai, 2001). The first task given to the testers was to type the entire alphabet. This was representative of the average speed that the users could find a character of the keyboard. The testers were then given a set of phrases to type. For a direct comparison, this set of phrases was the same as those used by Smith and Zhai.

The testers typed in 10 minute sessions once a day for a week. Figure 8 shows a graph of the average typing speed over these 7 sessions. The keyboard with the alphabetic bias performed around 10% better than the optimal keyboard for the first test. As the testing progressed, the performance on the optimal keyboard improved until it matched the alphabetic keyboard.

Based on the character frequency analysis, the optimal keyboard has a top typing speed 10% higher than the alphabetic keyboard. However, in an empirical test, novice users were able to type 10% faster on the alphabetic keyboard. The learning curve for the alphabetic keyboard was much quicker. The testers were able to find all of the characters on the alphabetic keyboard twice as fast as the optimal keyboard. On average, the testers found the keys in 10 seconds for the alphabetic keyboard and in 24 seconds for the optimal keyboard.

5 Assamese Keyboard Optimization

The Assamese language has more than twice the number of characters used in English. Hick's Law relates a users selection speed to the number of choices available(Hick, 1952). From this, we can assume that the efficiency is improved when a keyboard has fewer characters. We noticed that the Assamese language has two characters two represent each vowel. The vowel is written explicitly at the beginning of a word, but it is represented as a diacritic mark when used inside a word. We decided to create this distinction inside the user interface program instead of creating separate keys. When the user presses the vowel key, the appropriate symbol is displayed based on the context.

The specific keyboard shape for the single-input on-screen keyboard was a 8×7 square grid.

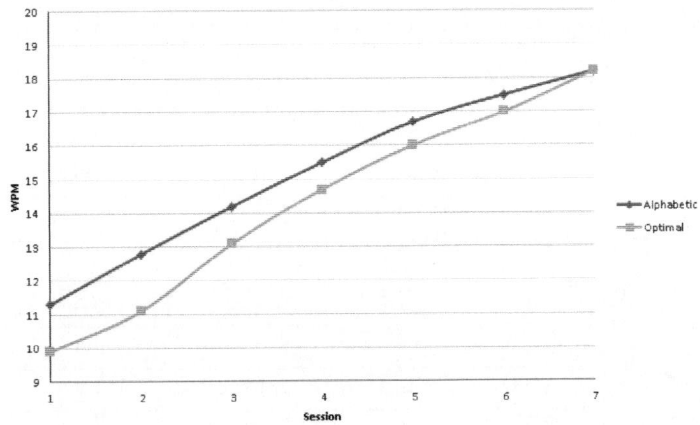

Figure 8: Results from human testing. The typing speed is an average computed from the results of 5 testers. During the early tests, a novice user was able to type around 10% faster using a the keyboard with alphabetic bias.

The two-input mobile keyboard was modeled as two QWERTY-shaped keyboards.

The large number of characters in the Assamese language made it difficult to determine the best method for grouping the characters for the ease of learning objective. We decided to create one group for the vowels and divide the consonants into 9 sub-groups based on the consonant rows. In order to determine the best combination of groups, we ran a series of tests to find the relation between the size of the groups and the predicted typing speed. Table 2 shows the results of these tests. There appears to be little variation in the typing speed between the different combinations of groups. The best results were achieved when the vowels were not grouped together. The combination of 4 groups appears to be the best compromise between group size and typing speed.

5.1 Optimization: Single-Input

Using the specifications above, we used the genetic algorithm to optimize the key positions. As with the English keyboard optimization, the optimized keyboard was generated from a population of 5000 solutions allowed to evolved over 20000 generations. The result was a pareto front containing 900 optimal solutions. For a representative solution, we selected the solution with the highest ratio (Objective 1/Objective 2). The evaluator reported this solution as having an estimated typing speed of 38.8 and an average distance of 1.6 keys between two characters in the same group(See Figure 9).

5.2 Optimization: Two-Input Mobile Keyboard

The next experiment involved generating an optimized mobile keyboard for the Assamese language. This test was run with a population of 5000 over 15000 generations. This test implemented the third constraint to eliminate groups being split between the two keyboards. For this test, we created 4 character groups to cluster for the second constraint. A representative solution had an estimated typing speed of 52 WPM and an average distance of 2 keys between two characters in the same group(See Figure 10).

# of Groups	Avg. Group Size	WPM	Avg. Group Dist.	Vowels Free
1	40.0	38.99	3.342	YES
1	26.0	38.29	2.632	NO
2	20.0	39.01	2.333	YES
2	17.3	38.43	2.333	NO
3	13.3	38.50	1.887	YES
3	13.0	38.07	1.917	NO
4	10.0	39.10	1.639	YES
4	10.4	38.46	1.759	NO
9	4.44	38.39	1.022	YES
9	5.20	38.01	1.190	NO

Table 2: Results of changing the number of groups.

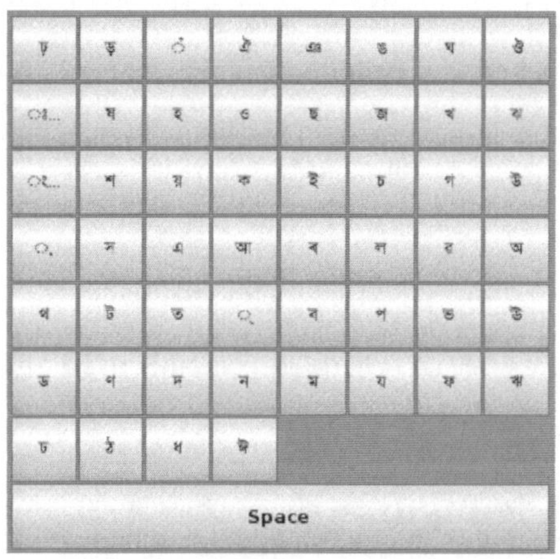

Figure 9: Optimized Assamese keyboard generated with a population of 5000 over 20000 generations. This layout has an estimated typing speed of 39 WPM and an average distance of 1.6 keys between two characters in the same group.

Keyboard	WPM
Flat alphabetic	25.1
Layered alphabetic	33.9
Flat GA-designed	34.2
Layered GA-designed	40.2
Flat multi-objective	38.8
Multi-objective mobile	52.0

Table 3: Comparison of our keyboards with those designed by (Hinkle et al., 2012).

Figure 10: Optimized Assamese keyboard generated with a population of 5000 over 20000 generations. This layout has an estimated typing speed of 52 WPM and an average distance of 2 keys between two characters in the same group. The evaluated alphabetic groups are highlighted.

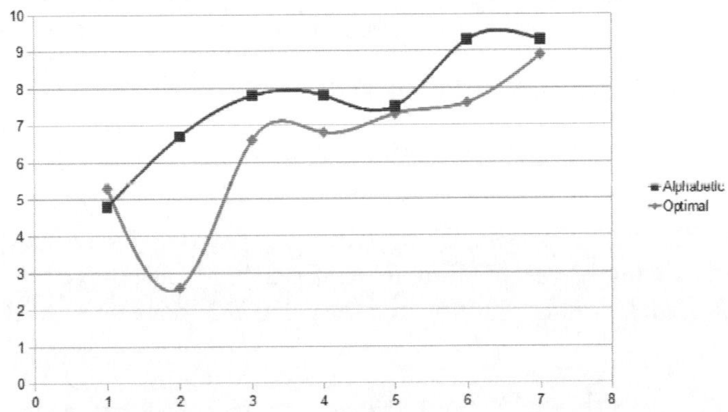

Figure 11: Preliminary results from human testing of the Assamese keyboards.

5.3 Human Testing

Under conditions identical to those in Section 4.4 , preliminary results were obtained from a single tester. While not as conclusive as the results for the English language, the graph in Figure 11 shows a similar pattern for the learning curve.

6 Future Work

The results reported for the performance of the English keyboards showed a significant improvement in early typing speeds for novice users. In order to make a conclusive comparison, the results reported for the Assamese language will need to be verified through additional human testing. Through the process of testing we hope to confirm the optimal number of character groups and the ease of learning. In order to facilitate the human testing process, we plan to make the keyboards available on-line for potential users to download. We also plan to make our mobile keyboards available on the Android market in return for user feedback on the usability of the keyboards.

Valuable information could be gained by optimizing keyboards for other languages. An interesting comparison could be made between the results for different languages. In the immediate future, a comparison could be made between the Assamese language and the Bengali language which shares the same character set.

Conclusion

The design of efficient user interfaces is critical for continued progress in human-computer interaction. The large number of variables in user interface design make it difficult to optimize interfaces. Multi-objective genetic algorithms provide a convenient method for optimization in applications that have a large number of constraints.

The use of multi-objective genetic algorithms was shown to produce very good results for creating optimized keyboards. An English keyboard designed after 20000 generations was able to double the efficiency of the unoptimized QWERTY keyboard for multiple constraints. Despite having twice the number of characters, an Assamese keyboard was generated that performed better than the QWERTY layout. Future work will validate the results discovered so far.

Acknowledgment

The work reported in this paper was supported by NSF Grant ARRA 0851783.

The authors would like to thank Devraj Sarmah for his assistance in testing the Assamese keyboards.

References

Ahlström, D., Cockburn, A., Gutwin, C., and Irani, P. (2010). Why it's quick to be square: modelling new and existing hierarchical menu designs. In *Proceedings of the 28th international conference on Human factors in computing systems*, CHI '10, pages 1371–1380, New York, NY, USA. ACM.

Clarkson, E., Clawson, J., Lyons, K., and Starner, T. An empirical study of typing rates on mini-qwerty keyboards. *CHI '05 extended abstracts on Human factors in computing systems*, pages 1288–1291.

Deb, K., Pratap, A., Agarwal, S., and Meyrivan, T. (April 2002). A fast and elitist multiobjective genetic algorithm: Nsga-ii. *IEEE Transactions on Evolutionary Computation*.

Fitts, P. (1954). The information capacity of the human motor system in controlling the amplitude of movement. *Journal of experimental psychology*, 47(6):381.

Gajos, K. Z., Weld, D. S., and Wobbrock, J. O. (2010). Automatically generating personalized user interfaces with supple. *Artificial Intelligence*, 174(12–13):910 – 950.

Hick, W. E. (1952). On the rate of gain of information. *Quarterly Journal of Experimental Psychology*, 4:11–26.

Hinkle, L., Brouillette, A., Jayakar, S., Gathings, L., Lescano, M., and Kalita., J. (2012). Design and evaluation of soft keyboards for brahmic scripts. *ACM Trans. Asian Language Inform. Process*.

Hinkle, L., Lezcano, M., and Kalita., J. (2010). Designing soft keyboards for brahmic scripts. *ICON 2010: International Conference on Natural Language Processing*, pages 191–200.

Konak, A., Coit, D. W., and Smith, A. E. (2006). Multi-objective optimization using genetic algorithms: a tutorial. *Reliability Engineering and System Safety*, 91:992–1007.

MacKenzie, I. and Soukoreff, R. (2002). A model of two-thumb text entry. In *Proceedings of Graphics Interface 2002*, pages 117–124. Toronto: Canadian Information Processing Society.

MacKenzie, I. S. (1992). Fitts' law as a research and design tool in human-computer interaction. *Human-Computer Interaction*, 7(1):91–139.

MacKenzie, I. S. and Zhang, S. X. (1999). The design and evaluation of a high-performance soft keyboard. In *Proceedings of the SIGCHI conference on Human factors in computing systems: the CHI is the limit*, CHI '99, pages 25–31, New York, NY, USA. ACM.

P. U. Lee, S. Z. (2004). Top-down learning strategies: Can they facilitate stylus keyboard learning? *International journal of human-computer studies*, 60(5-6):585–598.

Raynal, M. and Vigouroux, N. (2005). Genetic algorithm to generate optimized soft keyboard. In *CHI '05 extended abstracts on Human factors in computing systems*, CHI EA '05, pages 1729–1732, New York, NY, USA. ACM.

Smith, B. and Zhai, S. (2001). Optimal virtual keyboards with and without alphabetical ordering–a novice user study. In *Proceedings of the INTERACT 2001: Eight IFIP Conference On Human–Computer Interaction*, pages 92–99, Tokyo, Japan.

Zhai, S. (2004). Characterizing computer input with fitts' law parameters - the information and non-information aspects of pointing. *International Journal of Human-Computer Studies*, 61(6):791–809.

Zhai, S., Hunter, M., and Smith, B. A. (2000). The metropolis keyboard - an exploration of quantitative techniques for virtual keyboard design. *Proceedings of the 13th annual ACM symposium on User interface software and technology*, pages 119–128.

Using Collocations and K-means Clustering to Improve the N-pos Model for Japanese IME

Long Chen Xianchao Wu Jingzhou He
Baidu Inc. (Shenzhen and Tokyo)
{chenlong05,wuxianchao,hejingzhou}@baidu.com

Abstract

Kana-Kanji conversion is known as one of the representative applications of Natural Language Processing (NLP) for the Japanese language. The N-pos model, presenting the probability of a Kanji candidate sequence by the product of bi-gram Part-of-Speech (POS) probabilities and POS-to-word emission probabilities, has been successfully applied in a number of well-known Japanese Input Method Editor (IME) systems. However, since N-pos model is an approximation of n-gram word-based language model, important word-to-word collocation information are lost during this compression and lead to a drop of the conversion accuracies. In order to overcome this problem, we propose ways to improve current N-pos model. One way is to append the high-frequency collocations and the other way is to sub-categorize the huge POS sets to make them more representative. Experiments on large-scale data verified our proposals.

Keywords: Input Method Editor, K-means clustering, n-gram language model, collocation.

1 Introduction

In Japanese IME systems [1], Kana-Kanji conversion is known as one of the representative applications of NLP. Unfortunately, numerous researchers have taken it for granted that current NLP technologies have already given a fully support to this task and there are few things left to be done as research topics. However, as we go deeper to this "trivial" task, we recognize that converting from a romanized Hirakana sequence (i.e., users' input) into a mixture of Kana and Kanji sequence (i.e., users' expected output) is more difficult than it looks. Concretely, we are facing a lot of NLP research topics such as Japanese word/chunk segmentation, POS tagging, n-best decoding, etc. Existing algorithms dealing with these topics are challenged by the daily-updating and large-scale Web data.

Traditional n-gram word-level language model (short for "word n-gram model", hereafter) is good at ranking the Kanji candidates. However, by using the large-scale Web data in tera-bytes (TB), even bi-gram word-level language model is too large[2] to fit the memories (for loading the model) and computing abilities (for decoding) of users' personal computers (PCs). Dealing with this limitation, n-pos model (Kudo et al., 2011) was proposed to make a compression[3] of the word n-gram model. N-pos model takes POS tags (or word classes) as the latent variable and factorizes the probability of a Kanji candidate sequence into a product of POS-to-POS transition probabilities and POS-to-word

[1] The Japanese IME mentioned in this paper can be freely downloaded from: http://ime.baidu.jp/type/?source=pstop

[2] For example, using the 2.5TB data, the word n-gram model has 421 million 1-grams and 2.6 billion 2-grams.

[3] Indeed, as pointed out by one reviewer, n-pos model has its own benefits by organizing the semantically similar words and dealing with low frequency words. Thus, even the result n-pos model is smaller than word n-gram model, it is considered to be also bring accuracy improvements (Kneser and Ney, 1993; Mori et al.).

emission probabilities. This factorization makes n-pos model alike the well-known Hidden Markov Model (HMM). Since the number of POS tags is far smaller than the number of word types in the training data, n-pos model can significantly smaller the final model without deteriorating the conversion accuracies too much.

Compared with word n-gram model, n-pos model is good for its small size for both storing and decoding. However, the major disadvantage is that important word-level collocation information are not guaranteed to be kept in the model. One direction to remedy the n-pos model is to find those lost word-level information and append it. The other direction is to sub-categorize the original POS tags to make the entries under one POS tag contain as less homophonic words as possible. These considerations yielded our proposals, first by appending collocations and second by sub-categorizing POS tags. Experiments by making use of large-scale training data verified the effectiveness of our proposals.

This paper is organized as follows. In the next section, we give the formal definition of n-pos model and explain its disadvantage by real examples. In Section 3 we describe our proposed approaches. Experiments in Section 4 testify our proposals. We finally conclude this paper in Section 5.

2 N-pos Model and Its Disadvantage

2.1 N-pos model

For statistical Kana-Kanji conversion, we use $\mathbf{x}$ to express the input Hirakana sequence, $\mathbf{y}$ to express the output mixed Kana-Kanji sequence and $P(\mathbf{y}|\mathbf{x})$ to express the conditional probability for predicting $\mathbf{y}$ given $\mathbf{x}$. We further use $\hat{\mathbf{y}}$ to express the optimal $\mathbf{y}$ that maximize $P(\mathbf{y}|\mathbf{x})$ given $\mathbf{x}$. Based on the Bayesian theorem, we can derive $P(\mathbf{y}|\mathbf{x})$ from the product of the language model $P(\mathbf{y})$ and the Kanji-Kana (pronunciation) model $P(\mathbf{x}|\mathbf{y})$. This definition is also similar with that described in (Mori et al., 1999; Komachi et al., 2008; Kudo et al., 2011).

$$\begin{aligned}\hat{\mathbf{y}} &= \text{argmax} P(\mathbf{y}|\mathbf{x})\\ &= \text{argmax} P(\mathbf{y})P(\mathbf{x}|\mathbf{y})\end{aligned}$$

There are flexibilities in implementing the language model and the pronunciation model. Suppose the output $\mathbf{y}$ contains n words, i.e., $\mathbf{y} = w_1 ... w_n$. We use 1) product of word class bigram model and word class to word emission model as the language model, and 2) word-pronunciation unigram model as the Kanji-Kana model. That is,

$$P(\mathbf{y}) = \prod_{i=1}^{n} P(w_i|c_i)P(c_i|c_{i-1}) \tag{1}$$

$$P(\mathbf{x}|\mathbf{y}) = \prod_{i=1}^{n} P(r_i|w_i) \tag{2}$$

Here, c_i is the word class for word w_i (frequently corresponds to POS tags or inflected forms), $P(w_i|c_i)$ is the word generation probability from a word class c_i to word w_i, $P(c_i|c_{i-1})$ is the word class transition probability, r_i is the Kana pronunciation candidate for word w_i, and $P(r_i|w_i)$ is the probability that word w_i is pronounced as r_i. The optimal output $\hat{\mathbf{y}}$ (or even n-best list) can be effectively computed by the Viterbi algorithm (Viterbi, 1967; Huang and Chiang, 2005).

There are many methods for designing the word classes, such as unsupervised clustering, POS tags, etc. Following (Kudo et al., 2011), we designed the word classes by using the POS information generated by an open-source toolkit Mecab[4] (Kudo et al., 2004) which was developed for Japanese word segmenting and POS tagging. Since POS bi-gram model plays an essential role in Equation 1, we call it *n-pos model*. Specially, similar to (Kudo et al., 2011), we also use the following rules to determine a word class:

- the deepest POS tag layers (totally six layers) of the IPA POS system[5] was used;
- for the words with inflection forms, their conjugated forms and inflections are all appended;
- particles, auxiliary verbs, and non-independence content words[6] are all taken as independent word classes; and,
- high-frequency verbs, nouns except named entities, adjectives, suffixes, prefixes are all taken as independent word classes.

Since there are many special words that are taken as word classes, we finally obtained around 2,500 word classes.

Probabilities $P(w_i|c_i)$ and $P(c_i|c_{i-1})$ can be computed from the POS-tagged corpus by using the maximum likelihood estimation method. The Kanji-Kana pronunciation model $P(r_i|w_i)$ can be computed by first mining Kanji-Kana pairs from the Web and then estimate their probabilities in a maximum likelihood way. Since Mecab also assigns Kana pronunciations and POS tags to Japanese words simultaneously during performing word segmentation, we can simply estimate $P(r_i|w_i)$ using the Web corpus pre-processed by Mecab. That is, $P(r_i|w_i) = freq(r_i, w_i)/freq(w_i)$. Here, function $freq()$ returns the (co-)frequency of a word and/or a Kana sequence in the training data. In our IME system, besides our basic Kana-Kanji conversion dictionary, the Kanji-Kana pairs mined from the Web are individually taken as "cell dictionaries". That is, they are organized by their category such as “idioms", “actor names", and so on. These cell dictionaries are optimal to the users and they can download those dictionaries which fit their interests. We also use a log-style function based on the frequencies of the Kanji candidates to compute the weights of the Kana-Kanji pairs. The weights are used to determine the rank of the Kanji candidates to be shown to the users.

2.2 The disadvantage

The basic motivation for factorizing $P(\mathbf{y})$ into Equation 1 is to compress the word n-gram model into the production of a bigram n-pos model $P(c_i|c_{i-1})$ and an emission model $P(w_i|c_i)$. N-pos model is good for its small size and the usage of syntactic information for predicting the next word. However, compared with word n-gram model, the disadvantage is clear: the co-frequency information of w_{i-1} and w_i is not taken into consideration during predicting.

Figure 1 shows an example for intuitive understanding of the disadvantage. Suppose both w_{i-1} (gennshi/nuclear) and w_i (hatsudenn/generate electricity) are low-frequency words in the training corpus, yet w_{i-1} always appears together with w_i (or we say w_{i-1} and w_i form a collocation). Under n-pos model, the total score of w_{i-1} w_i is determined mainly by $P(c_i|c_{i-1})$ and $P(w_i|c_i)$, but not $P(w_i|w_{i-1})$. Thus, the best candidate “nuclear power” in word n-gram model is possibly not be able to be predicated as the top-1 candidate in n-pos model.

[4]http://mecab.sourceforge.net/

[5]http://sourceforge.jp/projects/ipadic/

[6]non-independent content words (such as oru, aru, etc.) are those content words that do not have an independent semantic meaning, but have to be used together with another independent content word to form a complete meaning.

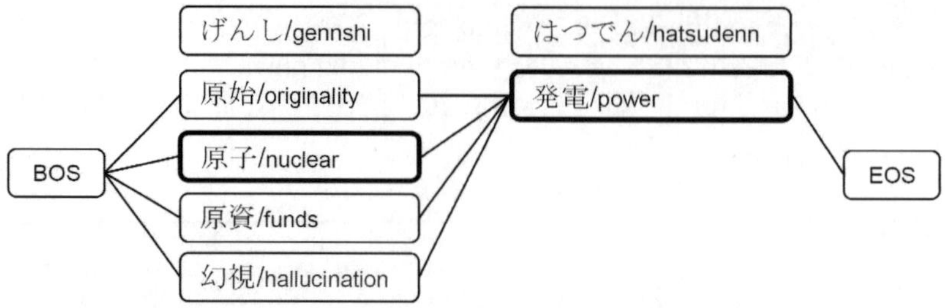

Figure 1: An example for the disadvantage of n-pos model.

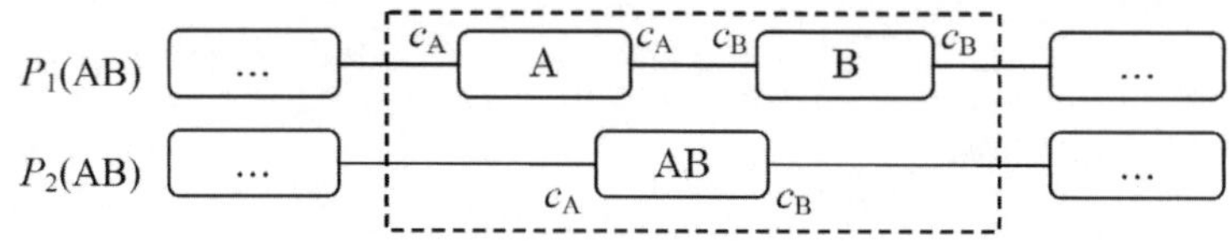

Figure 2: Changing n-pos model by replacing individual words *A* and *B* with collocation *AB*.

3 The Proposed Method

3.1 Appending "partial" word n-gram model

The disadvantage of n-pos model is mainly caused by its compression of word n-gram model. N-pos model can deal with a large part of the Kana-Kanji conversion problem yet short at dealing with collocations. We are wondering if partial of the word n-gram model can be "appended" to the n-pos model to further improve the final conversion precision.

The challenge is how to balance the usage of the two models for ranking the Kanji candidates. The score of a Kanji candidate sequence *AB* (with two words) can be computed by both the word n-gram model and the n-pos model. One simple consideration is to trust word n-gram model whenever n-pos model "fails" to make a better ranking. That is, we make use of word n-gram model only if candidate *AB* was assigned a higher score in word n-gram model than that in n-pos model.

We explain this idea through an example shown in Figure 2. In this figure, we want to replace individual words *A* and *B* in the decoding word lattice in the original n-pos model by a collocation *AB*, knowing that *A* and *B* sharing a high co-frequency in the training data.

$$
\begin{aligned}
P_1(AB) &= P(A|c_A)P(c_B|c_A)P(B|c_B) \\
&= \frac{freq(A)}{freq(c_A)} \times \frac{freq(c_A c_B)}{freq(c_A)} \times \frac{freq(B)}{freq(c_B)}; \\
P_2(AB) &= \frac{freq(AB)}{freq(c_A)}.
\end{aligned}
$$

Here, c_A and c_B stand for the POS tag (or word class) of word A and B; function $freq()$ returns the frequency of words and POS tags in the training data. When appending collocations to the n-pos model, we need to let $P_1(AB) < P_2(AB)$ to ensure the collocation candidate has a higher rank in the candidate set. That is,

$$\frac{freq(A)}{freq(c_A)} \times \frac{freq(c_B)}{freq(c_A)} \times \frac{freq(B)}{freq(c_B)} < \frac{freq(AB)}{freq(c_A)}, i.e.,$$
$$\frac{freq(A)freq(B)}{freq(c_A)freq(c_B)} < \frac{freq(AB)}{freq(c_A c_B)} \quad (3)$$

We make use of Formula 3 for mining collocations from the bi-grams in the training data.

There is one approximation in Formula 3. For collocation *AB*, its word class sequence is $c_A c_B$. When computing $P_2(AB)$, we only used $freq(c_A)$ instead of $freq(c_A c_B)$. Note that when computing the right-hand-side of *AB* in the second line, we still use c_B as the right-hand-side POS of *AB*. Similar strategy (of using c_A as the left-hand-side POS tag and c_B as the right-hand-side POS tag of *AB*) has been applied in Mecab and ChaSen[7] for Japanese word segmenting and POS tagging.

3.2 K-means clustering

The objective for unsupervised K-means clustering is to avoid (as much as possible) assigning entries with identical pronunciations or with large frequency variances into one word class. One big problem that hurts the precision of n-pos model is the existence of Kanji candidates with identical pronunciations in one word class, since the ranking is only determined by $p(w_i|c_i)$. If we could assign different word classes to the homophonic Kanji candidates, we can further make use of $P(c_i|c_{i-1})$ instead of only $P(w_i|c_i)$ to yield a better candidate ranking.

We define a kernel function[8] $F(A_1,A_2)$ to describe the difference of pronunciations between two Kanji candidates A_1 and A_2:

$$F(A_1,A_2) = \frac{1}{ed(pron(A_1), pron(A_2)) + 0.001} \quad (4)$$

Here, function $pron()$ returns the romanized Japanese Katakana sequence of a Kanji word[9]; function $ed()$ returns the edit distance of two string parameters. In this paper, we use the Levenshtein distance as defined in (Levenshtein, 1966). Through this definition, we know that the smaller the edit distance is, the larger value the $F()$ function returns. In case of A_1 and A_2 share an identical pronunciation, $F()$ returns the maximum value of 1,000. On the other hand, the bigger the edit distance, $F()$ is closer to 0. Thus, we say $F() \in (0, 1000]$.

Table 1 shows the top-5 high frequency pronunciations in our Kana-Kanji conversion lexicon. In this table, *yuuki* takes the highest frequency of 156. We thus set the K in K-means clustering to be 156 so that optimally all the 156 Kanji candidates with the pronunciation of *yuuki* can be assigned to some word class that is different from each other.

During K-means clustering, we first randomly pack 156 pronunciations as centre points from the Kana-Kanji conversion lexicon and then computer the distance score of $F()$ by using Equation 4. We aggressively assign one entry to the word class with the biggest $F()$ score.

[7] http://chasen-legacy.sourceforge.jp/

[8] As pointed out by one reviewer, this is not the only way to estimate the distance between to entries. Indeed, there are many personal names which should be taken as one special word class, we take this as an interesting future work.

[9] For example, in Figure 1, "gennshihatsudenn" is the result by applying $pron()$ to the Kanji candidates.

Pronunciation	Frequency	Kanji examples				
ユウキ/yuuki	156	雄喜	裕希	裕記	雄生	勇企
コウジ/kouji	149	紘治	甲児	小池	講じ	小路
コウキ/kouki	134	弘毅	興起	晃毅	幸喜	功喜
ヨシヒロ/yoshihiro	118	義洋	佳洋	愛弘	吉広	善廣
ヒロシ/hiroshi	102	広し	洋資	博至	啓	博四

Table 1: The top-5 high frequency pronunciations in our Kana-Kanji conversion lexicon.

Rank	Six level POS tags	#	%	Top-Kana freq.	Top-Kana
1	名詞 一般 * * * *	359,951	39.69%	28	コウキ/kouki
2	名詞 固有名詞 一般 * * *	78,752	8.68%	7	アイノウタ/ainouta
3	名詞 固有名詞 地域 一般 * *	75,190	8.29%	11	コウヨウ/kouyou
4	名詞 固有名詞 人名 名 * *	61,280	6.76%	132	ユウキ/yuuki
5	名詞 固有名詞 組織 * * *	60,489	6.67%	7	セイコウ/seikou
6	名詞 固有名詞 人名 一般 * *	49,704	5.48%	6	カトウヒロシ/katouhiroshi
7	名詞 固有名詞 人名 姓 * *	31,649	3.49%	14	ミナミ/minami
8	名詞 サ変接続 * * * *	12,919	1.41%	15	センコウ/sennkou
9	動詞 自立 * * 一段 連用形	6,177	0.68%	11	カケ/kake
10	動詞 自立 * * 一段 未然形	6,174	0.68%	11	カケ/kake
			81.83%	242	

Table 2: The top-10 high frequency six-level POS tags in our Kana-Kanji conversion lexicon.

There is one difficulty that we should mention here. Note that the edit distance function does not satisfies *triangle inequality*. That is, we cannot ensure $ed(A,B) < ed(A,C) + ed(C,B)$. This makes it a bit difficult to determine the new centre point in a word class. In our approach, instead of drawing the centre point by a determined string for the future computing of $F()$ for a given pronunciation string, we use the averaged $F()$ score from the given string to all the string in a word class as the *distance*. This modification changes the complexity of K-means clustering algorithm from $O(nKt)$ to $O(n^2Kt)$, where n is the number of entries in the Kana-Kanji conversion lexicon, K is the number of word classes, and t is the number of iterations.

In our preliminary experiments, we found that clustering on the whole conversion lexicon did not yield a better result. The major reason was that, we ignored the frequency information of the entries, POS tags, and pronunciations in the lexicon. That is, we should make a sub-categorization on the big POS sets, such as nouns, verbs, adjectives.

Table 2 lists the top-10 high frequency six-level POS tags[10] in our Kana-Kanji conversion lexicon which contains 907,003 entries. Note that the top-8 POS tags are nouns and occurs 80.47% of the lexicon. Table 2 also lists the most frequently appears Kana (i.e., pronunciation) in each of the POS set. If we independently run K-means clustering for each of the top-10 POS sets and take K to be the number of the top-Kata frequency, we will extend these 10 sets into 242 sets.

$$J = \sum_{i=1}^{K} \sum_{p \in c_i} \frac{\sum_{p' \in c_i} F^2(p, p')}{|c_i|} \tag{5}$$

[10] http://sourceforge.jp/projects/ipadic/

The objective function of the K-means clustering algorithm is shown in Formula 5. Here, c_i represents a word class, p and p' are word entries (with word, POS tag, and pronunciation) in c_i, and $F()$ function is defined in Equation 4.

4 Experiments

4.1 Setup

As mentioned earlier, we use 2.5TB Japanese Web pages as our training data. We run Mecab on Hadoop[11], an open source software that implemented the Map-Reduce framework (Dean and Ghemawat, 2004), for word segmenting and POS tagging the data. Then, based on maximum likelihood estimation, we estimate $P(c_i|c_{i-1})$, $P(w_i|c_i)$, and $P(r_i|w_i)$ (referring to Equation 1 and 2). Our foundational Kana-Kanji conversion lexicon contains 907,003 entries. Based on the reconstructing strategies described in Section 2.1, we initially obtained 2,569 word classes for these lexicon entries.

We report conversion accuracies on three test sets:

- 23Kw: this test set contains 23K common words that are manually collected from the Web (w is short for "word" level test set);
- 6Ks: this test set contains 6K sentences that are randomly collected from the Web as well (s is short for "sentence" level test set);
- 5Kw: this test set contains 5K words that are manually collected from the Web.

Specially, the 5K test set includes the following entries:

- 2.5K high frequency words that are collected from the Web;
- 1K common words that are randomly selected from Nagoya University's common word list[12];
- 0.5K basic concept verbs;
- 0.2K single Bensetsu (alike English chunk) words that are manually collected from the Web;
- 0.2K Japanese family names;
- 0.2K Japanese idioms;
- 0.2K Japanese place names;
- 0.2K Japanese single Kanji characters.

We use the following evaluation metrics:

- top-1/3/5 "precision", i.e., if the reference Kanji string is included in the 1(3/5)-best output list;

[11] http://hadoop.apache.org/

[12] http://kotoba.nuee.nagoya-u.ac.jp/jc2/base/list

Test set	System	Top-1	Top-3	Top-5	1st screen	Recall
23Kw	baseline	73.34%	90.30%	94.08%	96.75%	98.71%
23Kw	+collocations	**73.48%**	**90.58%**	94.23%	**96.91%**	**98.87%**
23Kw	+clustering	73.30%	90.57%	**94.24%**	96.86%	98.76%
23Kw	+collocations+clustering	73.40%	90.33%	94.06%	96.77%	98.81%
6Ks	baseline	66.36%	89.25%	91.77%	93.00%	93.68%
6Ks	+collocations	**68.56%**	90.50%	92.83%	93.97%	94.62%
6Ks	+clustering	66.71%	**91.77%**	**93.87%**	**95.38%**	**95.38%**
6Ks	+collocations+clustering	68.34%	90.02%	92.43%	93.53%	94.23%
5Kw	baseline	82.79%	93.07%	95.04%	96.48%	98.71%
5Kw	+collocations	82.84%	**93.62%**	**95.55%**	96.69%	**98.98%**
5Kw	+clustering	**82.88%**	93.54%	95.49%	**96.72%**	98.86%
5Kw	+collocations+clustering	**82.88%**	93.20%	95.27%	96.57%	98.92%

Table 3: The accuracies of appending collocations and K-means clustering. Here, w = word, s = sentence.

Word1	Word2	Kana1	Kana2
会社/company	情報/information	ガイシャ	ジョウホウ
人気/popular	商品/products	ヒトケ	ショウヒン
沖/oki, place name	地震/earthquake	オキ	ジシン
不動産/estate	会社/company	フドウサン	ガイシャ
半角/halfwidth	英数字/english letters, numbers	ハンカク	エイスウジ
生命/life	保険/ insurance	イノチ	ホケン

Figure 3: Examples of bi-gram collocations.

- first screen "precision", i.e., if the reference Kanji string is included in the first screen of the output list. Currently, we set the first screen includes top-9 candidates;
- "recall", i.e., if the reference Kanji string is included in the output list of the IME system.

By using the "precision" criteria, we hope to measure the goodness of the ranking of the output candidate list. The best situation is that, all the reference Kanji strings appear as the 1-best output of the IME system. Also, by using the "recall" criteria, we hope to measure the rate of missing Kanji candidates for the given input Kana sequences. A lot of Japanese family names or given names occur rarely even in the 2.5TB training data. However, we have to make sure they are included in the candidate list, since this significantly influences users' experience.

4.2 Appending Collections

We mined 423,617 bigram collocations by filtering the bigram set of the 2.5TB training data using Formula 3. Figure 3 shows several examples of collocations mined. Each entry in the collocation contains Kanji-style word sequence, POS tags, and Kana pronunciations. These entries are appended to our foundational Kana-Kanji conversion lexicon.

Table 3 shows the top-1/3/5 precisions, first screen precisions, and recalls achieved by the baseline and the baseline appended with collocations. From this table, we observe that in both test sets, the collocation appending approach achieved a better precision/recall than the baseline system. Also,

Input Kana	Reference Kanji	Our IME system (1-best)	Meaning
うさぎ	兎	うさぎ	rabbit
うけとり	受取	受け取り	receive
いりぐち	入り口	入口	entrance
いらいら	いらいら	イライラ	boredom
いのちをかける	命を懸ける	命をかける	risk one's life
いただく	頂く	いただく	accept/let's eat
いたす	致す	いたす	do
あなた	貴方	あなた	you
あさごはん	朝御飯	朝ごはん	breakfast
あげる	上げる	あげる	increase

Table 4: 10 examples in our test sets that reflects both the reference Kanji and the top-1 output of our IME system are acceptable results.

note that the first screen precisions already achieved more than 93% and the recalls achieved more than 93%. Through these accuracies, we believe that our current IME system has achieved an inspiring accuracy under these test sets.

Another interesting observation is that, there is a big jump (more than 10%) of the conversion accuracies from top-1 to top-3 precisions. We made an inside analysis of the cases that took the reference Kanji into the second or third positions of the final output. An important fact is that, a lot of entries in the test sets do take multiple forms (i.e., either Kana or Kanji sequences) as their appearances. In most cases, there are more than one candidates in the top-3 lists are acceptable to the real users. Table 4 lists 10 cases that take both the reference and the top-1 output of our IME system as acceptable results to the Kana inputs. Indeed, since the ranking of the candidates are mainly based on their frequencies in the 2.5TB training data, we believe the top-1 outputs generated by our IME system are more frequently used by most users and are more "commonly" used as habits. Thus, we believe the top-1 precision is a "conservative" estimation of the final precision and it is reasonable for use to also refer to the top-3/5 and first screen precisions to evaluate the improvements of our proposed approach.

Finally, the improvements on the 6Ks sentence level test set are much better than that achieved in the 23Kw and 5Kw word level sets. This reflects that appending of collections is more suitable for large-context input experience.

After appending bi-gram collocations, we also performed extracting collocations from Japanese single Bensetsu and several Bensetsus. The new accuracy (especially, Top-1 precision) in the sentence level test set was significantly better than current results. We wish to report the detailed techniques and results in our future publications.

4.3 K-means Clustering

By performing K-means clustering to the top-10 word classes, we finally obtained 2,811 word classes. After obtaining the new word class set, we retrained $P(c_i|c_{i-1})$ and $P(w_i|c_i)$ using the 2.5TB Web data.

The precisions and recalls by applying clustering to the baseline IME system are also shown in Table 3. From the table, we also obtained improvements on both precisions and recall. Also, the improvements on sentence level test set with richer context information are better than that achieved in the word level test sets.

We finally combined our two proposals together, i.e, modify the original n-pos model by both appending collocations and sub-categorizing of POS tags. However, as shown in Table 3, the final results did not show a further better result than either of the single approaches. The main reason is that, the word classes for the collocations were based on the POS tags before sub-categorizing. This makes the collocations not sensitive to the changes of fin-grained POS tags. One solution to this problem is to enlarge the POS tags in the Japanese POS tagger, i.e., replacing the original IPA-style POS tags with our fine-grained POS tags. Since we do not have a training set with fine-grained POS tags, we wish to make use of the Expectation-Maximization algorithm (Dempster et al., 1977) to solve this problem by taking the fine-grained POS tag set as latent variable. Similar idea has been implemented for PCFG parsing with latent variables (Matsuzaki et al., 2005). We take this as a future work.

5 Conclusion

We have described two ways to improve current n-pos model for Japanese Kana-Kanji conversion. One way was to append the high-frequency collocations and the other way was to sub-categorize the huge POS sets. Experiments on large-scale data verified our proposals. Our Japanese IME system that implemented these ideas is completely free and has been used by millions of users running both on Windows-style PCs and Android-style smart phones. Future work includes enrich the feature set for unsupervised clustering, such as using the statistics, especially the context information[13], from the large-scale training data.

Acknowledgments

We thanks the anonymous reviewers for their comments and suggestions for improving the earlier version of this paper.

References

Dean, J. and Ghemawat, S. (2004). Mapreduce: simplified data processing on large clusters. In *Proceedings of OSDI*.

Dempster, A. P., Laird, N. M., and Rubin, D. B. (1977). Maximum likelihood from incomplete data via the em algorithm. *Journal of the Royal Statistical Society*, 39:1–38.

Huang, L. and Chiang, D. (2005). Better k-best parsing. In *Proceedings of IWPT*.

Kneser, R. and Ney, H. (1993). Improved clustering techniques for class-based statistical language modeling. In *In Proceedings of the European Conference on Speech Communication and Technology (Eurospeech)*.

Komachi, M., Mori, S., and Tokunaga, H. (2008). Japanese, the ambiguous, and input methods (in japanese). In *Proceedings of the Summer Programming Symposium of Information Processing Society of Japan*.

Kudo, T., Komatsu, T., Hanaoka, T., Mukai, J., and Tabata, Y. (2011). Mozc: A statistical kana-kanji conversion system (in japanese). In *Proceedings of Japan Natural Language Processing*, pages 948–951.

[13]One reviewer also pointed out this, we express our thankfulness here.

Kudo, T., Yamamoto, K., and Matsumoto, Y. (2004). Applying conditional random fields to japanese morphological analysis. In Lin, D. and Wu, D., editors, *Proceedings of EMNLP 2004*, pages 230–237, Barcelona, Spain. Association for Computational Linguistics.

Levenshtein, V. (1966). Binary codes capable of correcting deletions, insertions, and reversals. *Soviet Physics Doklady*, 10:707–710.

Matsuzaki, T., Miyao, Y., and Tsujii, J. (2005). Probabilistic CFG with latent annotations. In *Proceedings of the 43rd Annual Meeting of the Association for Computational Linguistics (ACL'05)*, pages 75–82, Ann Arbor, Michigan. Association for Computational Linguistics.

Mori, S., Nishimura, M., and Itoh, N. Word clustering for a word bi-gram model. In *Proceedings of ICSLP 1998*.

Mori, S., Tsuchiya, M., Yamaji, O., and Nagao, M. (1999). Kana-kanji conversion by a stochastic model (in japanese). *Journal of Information Processing Society of Japan*, 40(7).

Viterbi, A. (1967). Error bounds for convolutional codes and an asymptotically optimum decoding algorithm. *IEEE Transactions on Information Theory*, 13(2):260–269.

phloat : Integrated Writing Environment for ESL learners

$YutaHayashibe^1$ $MasatoHagiwara^2$ $SatoshiSekine^2$
(1) Nara Institute of Science and Technology, 8916-5 Takayama, Ikoma, Nara, Japan
(2) Rakuten Institute of Technology, New York, 215 Park Avenue South, New York, NY
yuta-h@is.naist.jp, {masato.hagiwara, satoshi.b.sekine}@mail.rakuten.com

Abstract

Most of the past error correction systems for ESL learners focus on local, lexical errors in a post-processing manner. However, learners with low English proficiency have difficulties even constructing basic sentence structure, and many grammatical errors can be prevented by presenting grammatical phrases or patterns while they are writing. To achieve this, we propose an integrated writing environment for ESL learners, called *phloat* to help such users look up dictionaries to find semantically appropriate and grammatical phrases in real-time. Using the system, users can look up phrases by either English or their native language (L1), without being aware of their input method. It subsequently suggests candidates to fill the slots of the phrases. Also, we cluster suggested phrases with semantic groups to help users find appropriate phrases. We conduct subject tests using the proposed system, and have found the system is useful to find the right phrases and expressions.

KEYWORDS: Writing Environment, Input Method, English as a Second Language, Suggestion of Patterns, Clustering of Candidates, Predicate Argument Structure.

1 Introduction

In the increasingly globalized world, opportunities to communicate with people who speak non-native languages are also increasing. English has established its position as the *de facto* lingua franca for many fields such as business and academia. This makes a large number of people worldwide to communicate in English as English-as-a-second-language (ESL).

Writing in English poses special challenges for those people. The major difficulties for ESL learners include lexicon, grammar or phrases, as well as articles and prepositions. A large number of systems and methods have been proposed to aid ESL learners for different aspects. For example, ESL Assistant and Criterion (Chodorow et al., 2010) is choosing and/or correcting appropriate articles and prepositions. Systems to assist learners in choosing the right verbs are also proposed, e.g. (Liu et al., 2011).

However, most of the systems are helpful only for local lexical or grammatical errors, and we believe a phrasal suggestion is needed to improve the English proficiency of ESL learners. Indeed, through a study on Japanese ESL learners' compositions, we found a significant number of errors which could be avoided if the learner knows appropriate phrases. Two examples from the study are shown in Example (1) (with some modification for simplicity):

* The expense burden becomes your department.
* It's usually the delivery of goods four business days. (1)

The first sentence, whose original intention is "Your department is responsible for the expense," is strongly affected by the first language (L1) expression なります *narimasu*, whose literal translation is "become." The author of this sentence translates the Japanese phrase into English literally, resulting in an almost incomprehensible sentence. The second sentence, with the original intention "It usually takes four business days to deliver the goods," does not follow any basic English structures. The author is assumed to have completely failed to put the words in the right order, even though he/she was successful in choosing the right words "delivery of goods" and "four business days."

These types of errors are extremely difficult to detect or correct by conventional ESL error correction systems. It is because they involve global structures of the sentence, and malformed sentences hinder robust analysis of sentence structures. Instead of attempting to correct sentences after they are written, we focus on *preventing* these types of errors even before they are actually made. As for the first erroneous sentence shown above, the error could have been prevented if we could somehow present a basic pattern "X is responsible for Y" to the author and let the author fill in the slots X and Y with appropriate words and phrases. Similarly, presenting phrases such as "it takes X to do Y" to the author of the second one could have been enough to prevent him/her from making such an error. In order to achieve this, there is a clear need for developing a mechanism to suggest and show such phrases while ESL learners are composing sentences.

Figure 1: The response of input "okuru" (send)

We propose an integrated writing tool for ESL learners called *phloat* (PHrase LOokup Assistant Tool) to achieve this. The system is integrated within a text editor, and suggests English words and phrases based on the user input as shown in Figure 1. It also allows L1-based query input, i.e., if the user types a Romanized Japanese word, it shows all the words and phrases whose Japanese translations contain the query, as implemented also in PENS (Liu et al., 2000) and FLOW (Chen et al., 2012). In addition, the suggested phrases are classified and labeled based on their semantic roles (case frames). Figure 1 shows that, for an L1 input "okuru," which has several senses including "send something" and "spend (a life)," the system shows clusters of phrases corresponding to these senses. After the user chooses one of the phrases which contain slots to be filled, the system automatically shows suggestions for words which are likely to fit in the slots based on the context. This phrase clustering and slot suggestion help the user compose structurally more accurate, thus understandable English sentences.

We evaluate the effectiveness of our system based on the user experiments, where the ESL learners are asked to compose English sentences with and without the *phloat* system. The results were evaluated based on how grammatically accurate their English is (fluency), and how much of the original intention is conveyed (adequacy). Also the composition speed is measured. We will show that our system can help user find accurate phrases.

This paper is organized as follows: in Section 2, we summarize related work on English spelling/grammar correction and writing support systems. Section 3 describes the target, basic principle, and the design of our system. In Section 4, we describe the details of the implementation and the data we used. We elaborate on the experiment details in Section 5, and we further discuss the future work in Section 6.

2 Related Work

2.1 Post-edit Assistance Systems

There are a large number of post-edit systems for English spelling and grammar checking. ESL assistant, proposed by (Leacock et al., 2009) Web-based English writing assistance tool focused on errors which ESL learners are likely to make. It also shows parallel Web search results of the original and suggested expressions to provide the user with real-world examples. Criterion, developed by (Burstein et al., 2004) is another Web-based learning tool which uses an automatic scoring engine to rate the input learner's composition. It also shows detailed stylistic and grammatical feedback to the learner for educational purposes. Other than these, one can also find many other free or commercial English writing assistance systems including Grammarly[1], WhiteSmoke[2], and Ginger[3] to name a few. However, all these systems assume rather static input, i.e., focus on post-processing learners' compositions already finished. However, as stated in the previous section, many errors could be avoided by presenting appropriate feedback *while* the user is composing sentences.

2.2 Real-time Assistance Systems

Therefore, real-time assistance can be a more attractive solution for ESL error detection and correction. Recent versions of Microsoft Word[4] have a functionality to automatically detect spelling

[1] http://www.grammarly.com
[2] http://www.whitesmoke.com/
[3] http://www.getginger.jp/
[4] http://office.microsoft.com/en-us/word/

and elementary grammatical errors as the user types. AI-type[5] is an English input assistance software which helps users type at a higher rate by allowing partial matching of words. It also shows context-sensitive suggestions based on word n-grams.

PENS (Liu et al., 2000) is a machine-aided English writing system for Chinese users. Particularly noteworthy about the system is that it allows L1 (first language) input, that is, the system shows English translations for the user input in a Pinyin (Romanized Chinese) form. FLOW (Chen et al., 2012) is an English writing assistant system for Chinese, also allowing L1 input. Unlike PENS, FLOW further suggests paraphrases based on statistical machine translation to help users refine their composition. It is also helpful for writing in controlled natural languages to show real-time grammatical suggestions.

英文名文メイキング "Eibun Meibun Meikingu" (lit. meaning *Making excellent English*) (Doi et al., 1998) proposes an IME-type writing assistant for English. The system interacts with subsystems such as Japanese-English dictionary look-up, example sentence search, and *Eisaku Pen*, which converts Japanese input directly into English expressions. Google Pinyin IME[6] has support features for Chinese ESL learners, including integrated dictionary look-up, L1-based input support, and synonym suggestion. The same kind of L1-based dictionary look-up is also integrated in many IMEs, such as ATOK[7] and Google Japanese IME[8] for Japanese, Sogou[9], and Baidu Input Method[10] for Chinese. Some of those systems also support fuzzy matching with erroneous input, and suggestion of frequent phrases.

In a somewhat different line of research, controlled natural languages also benefit from writing support tools. AceWiki (Kuhn and Schwitter, 2008), which is a semantic wiki making use of a controlled natural language ACE, also provides an interactive writing support tool which automatically suggests subsequent word candidates as the user types.

Our proposal falls in this category. Compared to the previous systems, our tool is focus on phrase suggestion on top of the useful features developed in the past.

2.3 Phrase Search Systems

Phrase search plays an important role in English translation and composition. Several projects have been conducted for storing and searching useful English patterns such as "there is a tendency for [noun] to [verb]" (Takamatsu et al., 2012; Kato et al., 2008; Wible and Tsao, 2010). However, most of the phrase search systems require rather high level of English proficiency to use mainly targeted at technical writing. Also, they are not integrated in a text editor, or do not allow L1-based input, leaving a significant room for improvement when used in practice.

2.4 Translation Support System

ESL writing assistant is closely related to translation support systems because human translators often have to refer to a wide range of resources such as dictionaries and example sentences. To name a few of a wide variety of translation support systems, TransType2(Esteban et al., 2004) and TransAhead (Huang et al., 2012) suggest candidate words and phrases in the target language based

[5] `http://aitype.com`

[6] `http://www.google.com/intl/zh-CN/ime/english/features.html`

[7] `http://www.atok.com/`

[8] `http://www.google.co.jp/ime/`

[9] `http://pinyin.sogou.com/`

[10] `http://shurufa.baidu.com/`

on automatic translation of the source sentences. TWP (Translation Word Processor) (Muraki et al., 1994; Yamabana et al., 1997) is another translation tool which support composes the target sentence in an incremental and interactive manner.

3 Overview

3.1 Motivation

The proposed system aims to help users who are not necessarily good at English, especially in a writing form. For them, writing English is not an easy task; looking up dictionary, finding the right phrase, taking care of grammars and so on. It takes a lot of time for them to compose sentences. In such a situation, real-time assistance can be a promising help for them, because it saves a lot of their time spent on dictionary look-up. Additionally, because they may construct sentences based on L1 influences, the real-time assistance can prevent mistakes which may otherwise be difficult to correct by guessing what the users intended to say in the first place.

As we mentioned in Section 2, several systems have been proposed to address this issue. AI-type and FLOW suggest subsequent phrases based on n-gram statistics and machine translation, respectively. PENS and Google Pinyin IME suggest words corresponding to the L1 input.

However, these systems have two problems. First, they are not aiming at the users whose English proficiency is really low. As shown in Example (1), simple concatenation of partial translations does not necessarily produce grammatical sentences which express what they originally intended[11]. Second, although previous systems simply show candidates in a single column, it is difficult to find appropriate phrases when the number of candidates is really large.

In order to solve these problems, we propose an integrated writing environment for ESL learners called *phloat* (PHrase LOokup Assistant Tool).

3.2 System Overview

The proposed system works on a simple editor. Authors can write English sentences, as he/she does on a regular editor. Also, on top of English input, the author can type Romanized Japanese words when he/she does not know what to write in English. The system searches corresponding words in both languages, and displays the information in real-time.

For example, Figure 1 in Section 1 shows how the system supports when the user types "okuru" (which means "send" or "spend" in English). On its left, it displays the word translation candidates, and on its right (three columns in the figure), phrasal suggestions for "okuru" in three clusters are shown with Japanese translations. In this manner, the author can choose the appropriate word or phrase which matches the intent of the author.

If the author's intent is to write "sending email", the author can click the corresponding phrase (in the example, the second phrase of the first cluster of "okuru"). This action replaces the user input "okuru" with the corresponding English phrase "email the address of". As we know that we need to fill the slot of "address of", the system suggests the possible fillers of this slot (Figure 2).

The system works even the input is partial Japanese (Figure 3) or a part of English phrase (Figure 4). It also shows the suggestion for a combination of two Japanese words (Figure 5).

In the next subsection, we will summarize the notable features of the system.

[11] AceWiki indeed supports and ensures grammatical composition, although semantic consistency is not guaranteed.

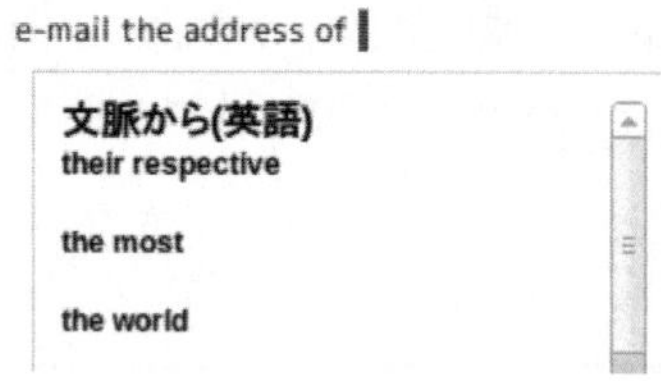

Figure 2: The suggestion for the slot in "okuru"

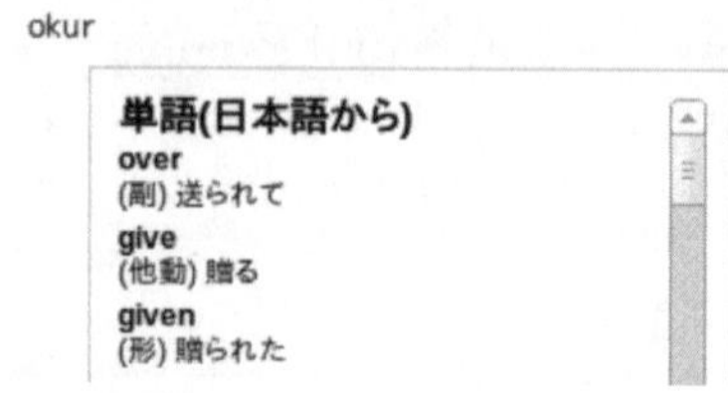

Figure 3: The response to input "okur" (A prefix meaning "send" in Japanese)

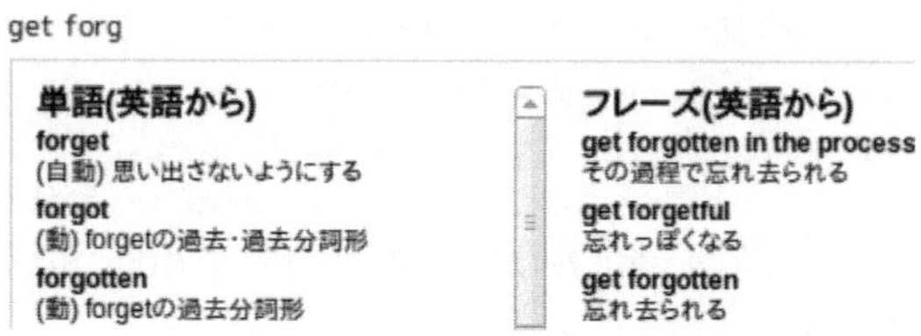

Figure 4: The response to input "get forg"

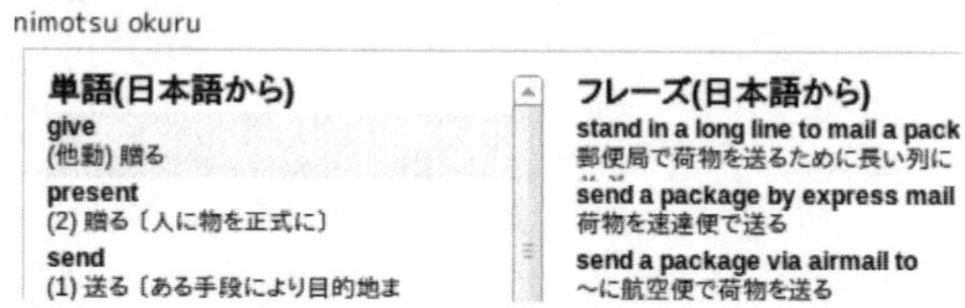

Figure 5: The response to input "nimotsu" (package) and " okuru" (send)

3.3 Features

Phrase Suggestion It suggests English phrases, on top of English words. As we have described, phrases could be better to be used in order to avoid unrepairable mistakes. Also, as the phrases are accompanied by Japanese sentences, the author may find the right phrase if it exists in the candidates. The phrases are semi-completed, natural phrases for native speakers like the ones shown in Table 2.

Slot Suggestion After the user chooses one of the candidate phrases, the system subsequently suggests candidates to fill in the slots of the phrase (Figure 2). These slot candidates are generated from the context of the suggested English phrase and its Japanese translation. This enables users to complete a long expression just by choosing a phrase and filling out the blanks in it.

Semantic Cluster Suggestion Since the system allows L1-based input in Romanized scripts, it results in a large number of phrase candidates which (probably partially) contain the L1 query, many of which belong to different semantic clusters. For example, Japanese verb "okuru" has at least two senses, "to send somebody something", and "to spend a life". Because our phrase list does not include sense knowledge, we need to group the phrases based on senses for the authors to find the appropriate one easily. The system suggests candidates with semantic groups (Figure 1), arranged it in multiple columns.

Flexible Input Words and phrases are suggested to the authors without being aware of their input methods; English or Romanized Japanese. Otherwise, the authors would have to switch their input method between the English direct input mode and the Japanese Kana-Kanji conversion mode, which is very laborious. The inputs in the Romanized Japanese are converted back to Kana phonetic characters (Figure 1) to find the candidates.

In addition, we implemented incremental search using the word prefix (Figure 3), making it unnecessary to type the complete words. This is the same for English input (Figure 4).

Search by Two Japanese Words In some cases, users would like to narrow down the phrases using two keywords, typically verbs and their arguments. For example, one can type "nimotsu okuru" (lit. package send) to narrow down phrases which are related to sending some packages, as illustrated in Figure 5.

4 Implementation

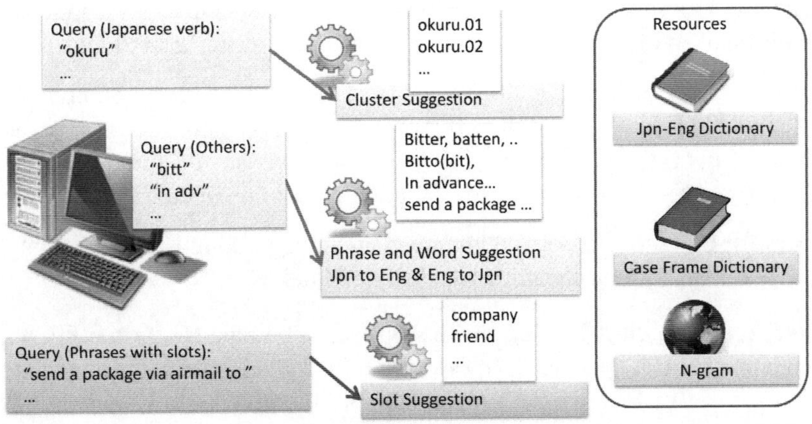

Figure 6: Overview of the System

4.1 System Components

We illustrate the overview of the system in Figure 6. The system is comprised of three components - Normal word/phrase look-up, cluster suggestion, and slot suggestion. Since the system is unable to know the type of query (Romanized Japanese or English) from the input character sequence in advance, the system executes all the following search procedures every time the user types a character. The system receives 30 characters surrounding the carets as a query, which is in turn used for dictionary lookup:

- Looking up by a prefix of a Japanese word in Romaji
  (e.g.) *hashi* → chopsticks (hashi), edge (hashi), post (hashira)...
- Looking up by a prefix of a Japanese phrase in Romaji
  (c.g.) *nimotsu* → carry an armload of packages (nimotsu wo yama no youni kakaete iru)...
- Looking up by a prefix of an English word
  (e.g.) *cong* → congregation, congenital, congressman...
- Looking up a by prefix of an English phrase
  (e.g.) *in adv* → in advance of ∼, in advanced disease...

After the look-up, all the results from each of the above search are shown. When the input is a Japanese verb, the phrases returned by the dictionary look-up are shown in semantic clusters. After the user chooses one of the phrases, the slot suggestion component is invoked to show suggestions.

All the components consult a Japanese-English dictionary. To achieve efficient look-up, all the entries in the dictionary are indexed with all the possible prefixes of their English translation and all the possible prefixes of tokens (except for particles) in Romaji of their sense in Japanese. For example, a phrase "carry an armload of packages" is indexed as shown in Table 1 [12].

	original string	prefixes
Japanese	nimotsu wo yama no youni kakaete iru	n, ni, nim, nimo, . . . , y, ya, yam, yama, . . .
English	carry an armload of packages	c, ca, car, carr, carry, carry a, carry an, . . .

Table 1: The Index of "carry an armload of packages"

[12]The variations, such as "ふ" (fu, hu) and "し"(shi, si) in Romanized forms of both Japanese senses and users input are all normalized by exploiting the Romaji table by Microsoft (`http://support.microsoft.com/kb/883232/ja`)

To avoid slow response and annoying users with too frequent suggestion, the first two searches (Japanese word/phrase look-up) are invoked only when the query is two or more characters long, and the last two are invoked only when the query is four or more characters long.

The system shows the set of lists, each of which is obtained from each component. The candidates in each list are sorted in a descending order of the language model score. That is, we simply ranked words depending on their unigram frequencies, and phrases on the language model score divided by the number of tokens in the phrase. We adopted stupid backoff (Brants et al., 2007).

To make it easier for users to choose a candidate even among a long list of too many candidates, the system groups them up by their meanings as described below.

Semantic Clustering Although it is ideal for the system to be able to cluster any phrases which match the user query, we simply performed clustering only for verbs because it is relatively easy to define what the "sense" of verb phrases are, given an appropriate lexical knowledge. Note that we could perform similar clustering on nouns as well using resources such as (Sasano and Kurohashi, 2009).

Clustering is performed only when the user inputs a Japanese verb such as "okuru," "nageru" using a case frame dictionary, which looks like the one illustrated in Table 3. The dictionary contains what kind of arguments each predicate takes, and the frequency is assigned to each argument meaning how often the argument is used in the case frame (predicate sense).

To each phrase including a single verb, we assigned a case frame[13] in the following way. First, we analyze the predicate argument structure of the phrase and obtain its arguments, by using a Japanese dependency parser, as stated below. We then sum up the frequencies of all the argument by consulting the case frame dictionary, if the analyzed case frame has any arguments. Finally we select the case frame with the highest frequency and assign it to the phrase.

For instance, the Japanese verb "送る" has two case frames, each of which corresponds to "to send" and "to spend", respectively, in the dictionary, and suppose we want to determine which case frame, 送る.1 or 送る.2. a phrase "メールを人に送る" (send an e-mail to a person) belongs to.

In the phrase, the predicate has two arguments, "メール" (mail) with accusative case and "人" (person) with dative case. The case frame 送る.1 has both of the arguments as its components, and its score is computed as the sum of their frequencies $(168 + 107022)$. On the other hand, the phrase only has one argument for the case frame 送る.2, which is "人," and its score will be the argument's frequency (80). Finally, because 送る.1 has a higher score than 送る.2, we regard the phrase belongs to the cluster 送る.1.

The system also suggests candidate to fill in the slot in phrases after the user selects a phrase in the suggested candidates. We describe how to obtain this below.

Slot Suggestion The system suggests candidates to fill in the slots in two ways.

First, it uses N-gram statistics to obtain commonly used phrases around the slots. Take a phrase "send a package via airmail to $\sim$" (〜に航空便で荷物を送る) for instance, which has "via airmail to" as the left context of the slot "$\sim$". We can obtain most common phrases which follow the words, e.g., "company," "friend," etc. by looking up the statistics.

We also use the right-hand-side context when available. The context length is limited by N, where N is the maximum length of N-grams contained in the database. Suppose that $N = 5$ and

[13] We discarded other phrases (e.g., phrases with two or more verbs) for clustering for simplicity

context $\cdots w_{-3}w_{-2}w_{-1}{\sim}w_1w_2w_3\cdots$ is given, we can look up the N-gram database by multiple queries like $w_{-3}w_{-2}w_{-1}**$, $w_{-2}w_{-1}**w_1$, and so on[14]. We merged the multiple sets of phrases obtained in this way, and sorted them in the order of their frequencies.

Second, it uses a case frame dictionary to obtain plausible nouns which are likely to be filled in the slots. Taking the same phrase "send a package via airmail to ∼" for example, the case frame can be assigned in the same way as we described previously using the Japanese translation, and we know that the slot "∼" has the accusative case (に *ni* case). Now we can look up the case frame dictionary and obtain the candidates using the case frame and the case, showing them in the order of frequency.

4.2 Data and pre-processing

Eijiro We used words and phrases contained in the Japanese-English dictionary Eijiro version 134 (released on May 23th 2012) [15]. This is a very large database of English-Japanese translations developed by the Electronic Dictionary Project. It can also be looked up at "Eijiro on the web"[16]. It is one of the most popular English dictionaries in Japan and it is accessed by over two million people in a month and searched over a billion times in a year[17]. It includes over 330,000 words, 1,434,000 phrases which contain no slots, and 256,000 phrases which contain one or more slots.

We automatically annotated the Japanese translations of phrases with part-of-speech tags using MeCab 0.994 [18] with IPA dictionary 2.7.0-2007080 [19] and parsed with dependency structures using CaboCha 0.64 [20].

In order to make the inversed index, we converted Japanese translations into Romaji, and obtained predicate argument structures. We regarded words which depend on a verb as arguments of the verb. Somc samplcs of thc predicate argument structure analysis are shown in Table 2.

Patterns	Predicate argument structures
～に関する質問を（人）に E メールで送る e-mail someone with one's questions regarding ∼	Verb: 送る Accusative:人 By:E メール
～のアドレスにメールを送る e-mail the address of ∼	Verb:送る Accusative:メール Dative:アドレス
～を E メールで送る send ∼ by e-mail	Verb:送る Accusative:∼ By:E メール

Table 2: Samples of Eijiro and their results of predicate argument structures analysis

Kyoto University's Case Frame We used Kyoto University's case frame data (KCF) ver 1.0 (Kawahara and Kurohashi, 2006)[21] as a Japanese case frame dictionary for slot suggestions and clustering. KCF is automatically constructed from 1.6 billion Japanese sentences on the Web. Each case frame is represented by a predicate and a set of its case filler words. It has about 40,000 predicates and 13 case frames on average for each predicate. We show some entries in KCF at Table 3.

Web 1T 5-gram We used Web 1T 5-gram Version 1 [22] which includes unigrams to five-grams collected from over 95 billion sentences on the Web for two purposes, for slot suggestion and

[14] Here $*$ denotes a wildcard.
[15] http://www.eijiro.jp/
[16] http://www.alc.co.jp/
[17] http://eowp.blogspot.jp/2011/12/on-web2011.html
[18] https://code.google.com/p/mecab/
[19] http://sourceforge.jp/projects/ipadic/
[20] https://code.google.com/p/cabocha/
[21] http://www.gsk.or.jp/catalog/GSK2008-B/catalog_e.html
[22] http://www.ldc.upenn.edu/Catalog/CatalogEntry.jsp?catalogId=LDC2006T13

送る.1	nominative	人:168, 私:152, ファン:89, 観客:80, 皆:73, < 数量 > 人:71, 誰:70, …
	accusative	メール:107022, メッセージ:34957, エール:14356, 情報:14048, 写 9047, …
	dative	方:3024, 友達:2679, アドレス:2492, 携帯:1704, 人:1557, 客:1443, < 数量 >9,
送る.2	nominative	人:80, 人々:62, 子供:55, 生徒:55, 学生:41, 自分:35, 方:29…
	accusative	生活:101316, 人生:19631, 余生:2001, 暮らし:1563, 寮生+活:57 …
	dative	実際:39, < 補文 >:38, 基:19, 風:16, 通り:12, よう:11, 中:10, 普通:10, 中心:8…

Table 3: Entries of Kyoto University's case frame data

candidate ranking, as discussed previously. For slot suggestion, we eliminates candidates which include symbols such as ".", "?", and "$< /S >$". We indexed this with Search System for Giga-scale N-gram Corpus (SSGNC) 0.4.6 [23] to achieve fast look-up.

5 Evaluation

5.1 Methods

We conducted user experiments to evaluate the effectiveness of the proposed system. The subjects for the user test are 10 Japanese ESL learners whose English proficiency is intermediate level. Their English proficiency is measured by TOEIC [24] score, and their average TOEIC score was 754. We showed them two sets of English composition problems consisting of e-mail response writing, free picture description, and Japanese-to-English translation, and asked the subjects to write answer English sentences with and without using the proposed system. The problem sample is shown below (the actual problems were presented in Japanese):

We chose the two pictures shown in Problem 2 from the ones at Flickr [25] with a CC (Creative Commons) License, making sure that the pictures somehow involve states/actions of animals[26] and humans[27]. The sentences in Problem 3 were chosen randomly from Tatoeba project[28], excluding too simple or too complex sentences.

Instruction

- Please answer the following problems and write English sentences USING THE SYSTEM. (For the system group)
- Please answer the following problems and write English sentences WITHOUT using the system. You can use your favorite editors or word processor software, unless they have spell check functionality. You can freely consult any Japanese-English / English-Japanese dictionaries, such as "Eijiro on the web"[29]. (For the baseline group)

Problem 1: E-mail composition You placed an order for a bag from an oversea shopping website. But you found out that the item was partially broken and had some stains on it, and would like to exchange it for a new one or to return it. Fill in the blank below and complete the e-mail. Your composition will be evaluated in terms of: 1) how accurate your choice of English words and grammar is, and 2) your intension is conveyed to the recipient in full.

[23] http://code.google.com/p/ssgnc/
[24] https://www.ets.org/toeic
[25] http://www.flickr.com/
[26] http://www.flickr.com/photos/tjflex/233574885/
[27] http://www.flickr.com/photos/yourdon/3386629036/
[28] http://tatoeba.org/
[29] http://www.alc.co.jp/

Problem 2: Picture description Please describe the following picture using five or less English sentences. Your composition will be evaluated in terms of: 1) how accurate your choice of English words and grammar is, and 2) how accurately the reader of your description can reconstruct the original image.

Problem 3: Japanese-English translation Please translate the Japanese sentences in Table 4 into English. Your translation will be evaluated in terms of 1) how accurate your choice of English words and grammar is, and 2) how much of the original Japanese meaning is preserved.

Japanese	A sample of translation
彼はローマに行ってたくさんの古い建物を見た。	He went to Rome, where he saw a lot of old buildings.
彼女は約束を破ったといって彼を責めた。	She accused him of having broken his word.
この本はかつてはベストセラーだったが、今は絶版になっている。	This book, which was once a best seller, is now out of print.
紫のじゅうたんはこの赤いカーテンと調和しないだろう。	A purple carpet will not go with this red curtain.
誰かが間違って私のかさを持っていったに違いない。	Someone must have taken my umbrella by mistake.

Table 4: Japanese sentences of Problem 3

5.2 Scoring

We prepared two identically structured problem sets with different contents, and also divided the subjects into two groups with their TOEIC average scores as closer as possible. We asked the former group to solve Problem Set 1 with the system and Problem Set 2 without the system. This order is inverted for the latter group, i.e., they solve Problem Set 1 without the system and Problem Set 2 with the system, to cancel out the learning effect. We also measured the time taken to complete each problem set.

After completion of the test, we asked two native speakers of English to grade the subjects' composition. The grading was based on two measures, fluency and adequacy, which is done for each problem (each sentence for Problem 3), based on the following rubric:

Fluency How grammatically accurate the sentence is as English (in terms of grammar, word choice, etc.) (This only looks at grammaticality. For example, writing "how are you?" to describe a picture does not make any sense, but it is completely grammatical, so Fluency will be 5.)

Rating	Description
5	fluent (native-speakers can write this kind of sentences, possibly with some unnaturalness or awkwardness)
4	completely acceptable (the meaning is understandable with few errors; non-nativeness can be suspected)
3	acceptable (the meaning is understandable, the structure follows basic English grammar, with some non-critical errors e.g., spelling errors, articles, prepositions, word choices etc.)
2	unacceptable (have some (possibly partial) serious errors which may make comprehension difficult e.g., non-existent words, basic word order, etc.)
1	completely unacceptable (the form of the sentence has serious flaws which may make comprehension impossible)

Table 5: Criterion of rating fluency

Adequacy How much of the original intention is conveyed. (This only looks information. For example, writing "on floor cat" is not grammatical at all, but it might be enough to convert the meaning "there's a cat on the floor." In this case, some insignificant information is dropped, like number and tense, so adequacy will be 4)

The final fluency/adequacy score is calculated as the weighted average of each score, with Problem 1 being weighted by a coefficient of 2.0 and Problem 2 by 5.0. Finally, we also asked the subjects for any feedback and comments on the system usability.

Rating	Description
5	full information conveyed (80%-100% of the original information is conveyed. The originally intended sentence can be reconstructed by simple paraphrasing)
4	most information conveyed (60%-80%)
3	half of information conveyed (40%-60%, including opposite meaning, e.g., dropped 'not' etc.)
2	some information conveyed (20%-40%)
1	almost no information conveyed (0%-20%)

Table 6: Criterion of rating adequacy

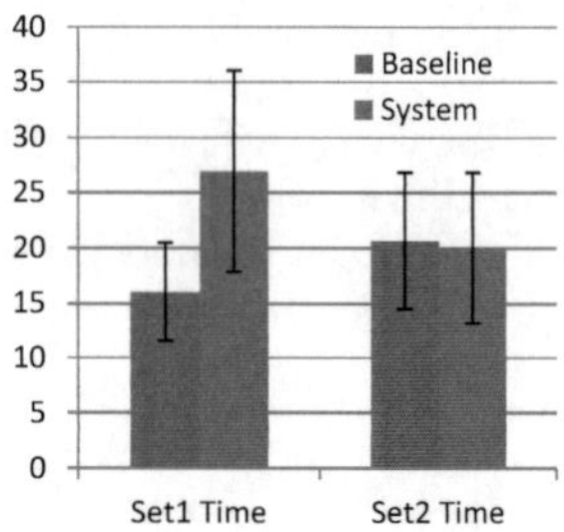

Figure 7: Comparison of the averaged time (minute)

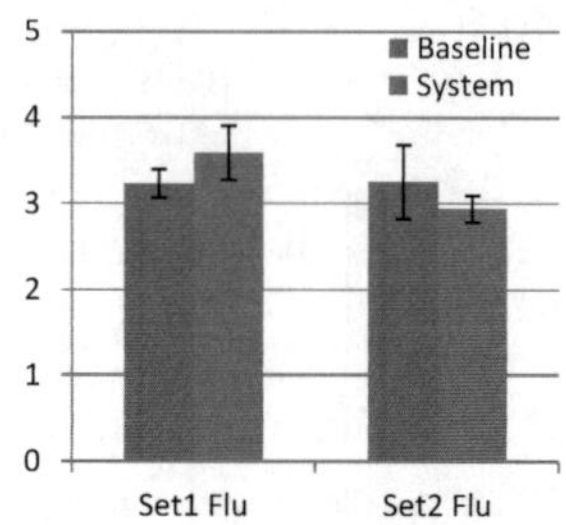

Figure 8: Comparison of the averaged fluency

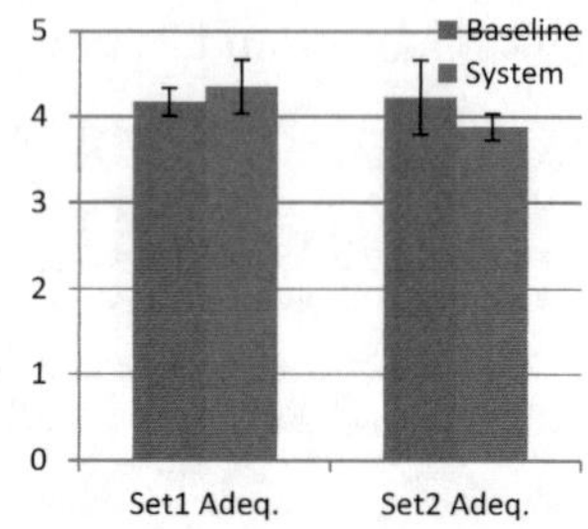

Figure 9: Comparison of the averaged adequacy

5.3 Results

Figure 7 compares the time taken to finish each problem set when the system is used ("System") and not used ("Baseline"). The result is mixed, where it took a far more amount of time for Problem Set 1 when the system is used, while it shows little difference for Problem Set 2. In particular, we observed a few subjects find difficulties getting used to using the *phloat* system, doubling the time taken to complete the test. This shows that, although the system is designed to be as intuitive as possible, the familiarity with the system greatly affects one's writing efficiency, and this leaves us some room for improvements in terms of both user interface and word/phrase search relevancy.

Figure 8 and 9 compare the overall fluency and adequacy scores for both System and Baseline. Again, the result is mixed, where System is scoring higher for Problem Set 1 while Baseline is scoring higher for Set 2.

Some subjects claimed that it reduced their burden that they can easily look up some unfamiliar word such as ぶち *buchi* (spotted, tabby) using the system, which obviously reduced the time and/or helped increase the fluency.

On the other hand, after analyzing the result in detail, we found that there is one particular problem which scored badly on average for System, which is to translate the following sentence into English: "彼女は約束を破ったといって彼を責めた。" (She accused him of having broken his word.) The answers which the System subjects wrote for this problem include: " * She pilloried him to break faith with her." and " * She berate him to break faith with her." Both "pillory somebody for ..." and "berate someone for ..." come up as the search result for a query "semeru" (accuse), even though they are somewhat rare expressions to describe the original intention. Apparently, the users without enough English proficiency had no clues to decide which candidates are the most appropriate ones, resulting in non-optimal word choices. This phenomenon was also seen for a problem where subjects are required to translate "屈する" *kussuru* (be beaten, submit to). Some chose inappropriate word "bow" which came up as the first result. Notice that this problem can also happen when learners consult general dictionaries, and the fact that the *phloat* system facilitates the dictionary look-up made the issue even worse.

5.4 Advantages of the System

From the evaluation of the system by the ESL learners, we found several examples where the system was very helpful.

Change the time of meeting to X o'clock This phrase can be found in the phrase candidates when the user search "kaigi (meeting)" and "henkou (change)". This problem made one of the biggest differences between the results by the subjects who used the tool and the results by the subjects who did not use the tool. 4 out of 5 subjects who used the tool wrote this or similar phrases, whereas the subjects who did not use the tool wrote the followings: "change the meeting from 11am" (does not say "time of the meeting"), "alter the starting time to 11am", or expressed in very awkward structure although we can capture the meaning. It is evident that people had difficult time to construct the sentences without suggestions. This proves that if the system shows the phrases which exactly matches the intent, the tool is quite useful.

Wasteful expenses/spendings by the government This phrase and its variant are used by three subjects who used the tool. It is one of the phrase candidates when you search "shishutu (expense)" and "muda (waste)". This phrase also seems a difficult one to make by the subjects without the tool, maybe because it is a terminology in a special domain.

Comply with the advice We believe this phrase is not very easy for Japanese subjects to come up with, but the system suggests it when you search "shitagau (comply)" and "chukoku (advice)". Most subjects without the tool wrote "follow the advice", which is perfectly OK, but it is an interesting discovery for us that the tool could be useful to extend one's vocabulary by suggesting unfamiliar words.

6 Future Work

6.1 Flexible Match

In the current system, nothing is shown when the system cannot find any phrases which match input queries. It is mainly because the current system requires an exact match, not because the coverage of the Eijiro is limited. Even word variations, such as plural, past-tense and so on are not handled. It could increase the number of matched phrases by including word variance match, and we believe a proper ranking system is needed if it causes a problem. When there is no match, we may want to try fuzzy matching. It is very likely that the ESL learners may not remember the spelling correctly, the fuzzy matching can be helpful. In order to increase the number of the prepared phrases, adding sentences generated by machine translation may also be useful. However, it requires us to judge the accuracy of the candidates. Related research on interactive translation is conducted by (Kim et al., 2008; Tatsumi et al., 2012).

6.2 Fine Grained Selection

The subtle nuances of phrases are very difficult for ESL learners. Examples include "home" and "house," "at last" and "finally," and "must" and "have to." It may be difficult for the system to solve it by the context. One idea to solve the problem is that the system asks the author by showing some examples which use such phrases.

6.3 Smarter Suggestion using Contexts

The current system only looks at the keywords up to two words, and more context aware mechanism might be helpful to make smarter suggestions.

For example, a proper part-of-the-speech can be guessed based on the context. For queries after a verb such as "I stopped *okuru nimotsu (send package)*", noun phrases should be more likely than verb phrases. Or following "have" or auxiliary verb, past participle or basic forms of verbs are most suitable, respectively.

The choice of prepositions is very difficult task for ESL learners, because the choice is depending on the context (type of verbs and the role of fillers), and influenced by the L1 of the user. For example, the phrase "is covered" should be followed by "by" if the sentence is "the accident is covered by insurance", but by "with" if the sentence is "the mountain is covered with snow", even though the Japanese particles in both cases are the same.

Sometimes, we have to take into account collocations of phrases. For example, a Japanese word "ookii" can be translated into "large," "many" or "big," and the appropriate choice of the word must be done by considering the modified noun. For instance, large is the best modifier for population than theres. In order to suggest the right adjective, the system needs to consider the collocation.

6.4 Better Ranking Algorithm

The order of candidates in the suggestion list is very important, as the users,look at it from the top of the list. The current system gives ranks words and phrases based on the language model scores or frequencies of the candidates themselves (without sense or context into consideration).

For a Japanese word "Umi" (the main sense is "sea"), the dictionary lists "blue" as one of its senses (very minor usage in Japanese). However, because the frequency of "blue" in the English corpus is larger than that of "sea", the current system suggest "blue" at the highest rank. In order to avoid the problem, we need to have knowledge of major or minor senses for each word.

Conclusion

In this paper, we proposed an integrated writing tool for ESL learners, called *phloat* (PHrase LOokup Assistant Tool). It helps users who are not necessarily good at writing English with looking up words and phrases in a dictionary. Presenting appropriate phrases while the author is writing prevents from making serious mistakes which can't be fixed at post processing.

Our main contributions are the followings.

First, phrase suggestion is incorporated. These phrases can be searched by either English or Romanized Japanese, by one or more keywords. The users can easily find popular phrases, which are accompanied with the translation in their native language. In addition, it subsequently suggests candidates to fill the slots of the phrases. These suggestions enable users to complete a sentence just by choosing a phrase and fillers of the slots.

Second, we proposed clustering of suggested candidates with semantic groups. L1-based input sometimes results in a large number of phrase candidates. This helps users to find related phrases very easily.

Lastly, we evaluated the system asking subjects to write English sentences with or without the tool. It proved that the tool is quite useful when the system shows the phrases which exactly matches the intent and helpful to extend one's vocabulary by suggesting unfamiliar words.

References

Brants, T., Popat, A. C., Xu, P., Och, F. J., and Dean, J. (2007). Large Language Models in Machine Translation. In *Proceedings of the 2007 Joint Conference on Empirical Methods in Natural Language Processing and Computational Natural Language Learning*, pages 858–867.

Burstein, J., Chodorow, M., and Leacock, C. (2004). Automated essay evaluation: the criterion online writing service. *AI Magazine*, 25(3):27–36.

Chen, M., Huang, S., Hsieh, H., Kao, T., and Chang, J. S. (2012). FLOW: A First-Language-Oriented Writing Assistant System. In *Proceedings of the 50th Annual Meeting of the Association for Computational Linguistics System Demonstrations*, pages 157–162.

Chodorow, M., Gamon, M., and Tetreault, J. (2010). The Utility of Article and Preposition Error Correction Systems for English Language Learners: Feedback and Assessment. *Language Testing*, 27(3):419–436.

Doi, S., Kamei, S.-i., and Yamabana, K. (1998). A text input front-end processor as an information access platform. In *Proceedings of the 36th Annual Meeting of the Association for Computational Linguistics and 17th International Conference on Computational Linguistics - Volume 1*, pages 336–340.

Esteban, J., Lorenzo, J., Valderrábanos, A. S., and Lapalme, G. (2004). TransType2: an innovative computer-assisted translation system. In *Proceedings of the ACL 2004 on Interactive poster and demonstration sessions*, pages 94–97.

Huang, C.-c., Yang, P.-c., Chen, M.-h., Hsieh, H.-t., Kao, T.-h., and Chang, J. S. (2012). TransAhead: A Writing Assistant for CAT and CALL. In *Proceedings of the Demonstrations at the 13th Conference of the European Chapter of the Association for Computational Linguistics*, pages 16–19.

Kato, Y., Egawa, S., Matsubara, S., and Inagaki, Y. (2008). English Sentence Retrieval System Based on Dependency Structure and its Evaluation. In *Third International Conference on Digital Information Management*, pages 279–285.

Kawahara, D. and Kurohashi, S. (2006). Case Frame Compilation from the Web using High-Performance Computing. In *Proceedings of the 5th International Conference on Language Resources and Evaluation*, pages 1344–1347.

Kim, C. H., Kwon, O.-W., and Kim, Y. K. (2008). What is Needed the Most in MT-Supported Paper Writing. In *Proceedings of the 22nd Pacific Asia Conference on Language, Information and Computation*, pages 418–427.

Kuhn, T. and Schwitter, R. (2008). Writing Support for Controlled Natural Languages. In *Proceedings of the Australasian Language Technology Association Workshop 2008*, pages 46–54.

Leacock, C., Gamon, M., and Brockett, C. (2009). User input and interactions on Microsoft Research ESL Assistant. In *Proceedings of the Fourth Workshop on Innovative Use of NLP for Building Educational Applications*, pages 73–81.

Liu, T., Zhou, M., Gao, J., Xun, E., and Huang, C. (2000). PENS: A Machine-aided English Writing System for Chinese Users. In *Proceedings of the 38th Annual Meeting of the Association for Computational Linguistics*, pages 529–536.

Liu, X., Han, B., and Zhou, M. (2011). Correcting Verb Selection Errors for ESL with the Perceptron. In *Computational Linguistics and Intelligent Text Processing*, pages 411–423.

Muraki, K., Akamine, S., Satoh, K., and Ando, S. (1994). TWP: How to Assist English Production on Japanese Word Processor. In *Proceedings of the 15th conference on Computational linguistics*, pages 847–852.

Sasano, R. and Kurohashi, S. (2009). A Probabilistic Model for Associative Anaphora Resolution. In *Proceedings of the 2009 Conference on Empirical Methods in Natural Language Processing*, pages 1455–1464.

Takamatsu, Y., Mizuno, J., Okazaki, N., and Inui, K. (2012). Construction of phrase search system for wiring english (in japanese). In *Proceedings of 18th Annual Meeting of The Association for Natural Language Processing*, pages 361–364.

Tatsumi, M., Hartley, A., Isahara, H., Kageura, K., Okamoto, T., and Shimizu, K. (2012). Building Translation Awareness in Occasional Authors: A User Case from Japan. In *Proceedings of the 16th Annual Conference of the European Association for Machine Translation*, pages 53–56.

Wible, D. and Tsao, N.-L. (2010). StringNet as a Computational Resource for Discovering and Investigating Linguistic Constructions. In *Proceedings of the NAACL HLT Workshop on Extracting and Using Constructions in Computational Linguistics*, pages 25–31.

Yamabana, K., Kamei, S.-i., Muraki, K., Doi, S., Tamura, S., and Satoh, K. (1997). A hybrid approach to interactive machine translation: integrating rule-based, corpus-based, and example-based method. In *Proceedings of the Fifteenth international joint conference on Artifical intelligence - Volume 2*, pages 977–982.

Phonetic Bengali Input Method for Computer and Mobile Devices

Khan Md. Anwarus Salam[1] *Setsuo Yamada*[2] *Tetsuro Nishino*[1]
(1) The University of Electro-Communications, Tokyo, Japan.
(2) NTT Corporation, Tokyo, Japan.
salamkhan@uec.ac.jp, yamada.setsuo@lab.ntt.co.jp, nishino@uec.ac.jp

ABSTRACT

Current mobile devices do not support Bangla (or Bengali) Input method. Due to this many Bangla language speakers have to write Bangla in mobile phone using English alphabets. During this time they used to write English foreign words using English spelling. This tendency also exists when writing in computer using phonetically input methods, which cause many typing mistakes. In this scenario, computer transliteration input method need to correct the foreign words written using English spelling. In this paper, we proposed a transliteration input method for Bangla language. For English foreign words, the system used International-Phonetic-Alphabet(IPA)-based transliteration method for Bangla language. Our proposed approach improved the quality of Bangla transliteration input method by 14 points.

KEYWORDS : Foreign Words, Bangla Transliteration, Bangla Input Method

1 Introduction

Bengali or Bangla is the official language of Bangladesh. Currently Bangladesh has 72.963 million mobile phone users. It is important to have Bengali input method for this huge number of Bengali language speakers. Although Bangladesh government declared standard keyboard layout for both computer and mobile device, currently there is no national standard for transliteration using English alphabets. Due to this there are many ambiguities in mapping 50 Bengali letters using 26 English letters. Different people have different assumptions on phonetic input system for Bengali language using English letters. These ambiguities effect the human communication, using mobile or emails, where people had no other choice except using English letters to write Bengali messages.

In this kind of scenario most people used to write English foreign words using English spelling. These ambiguities effect the human communication using SMS or email. In this kind of scenario most people used to write English foreign words using English spelling. To understand this kind of message needs a sophisticated phonetic input method for mobile devices. Bengali also needs a standard transliteration mechanism considering these issues. Such a transliteration scheme should be simple rule-base to minimize the computational resources.

In this paper, we propose a phonetic Bengali input method for computer and mobile devices. Our approach is a pattern-based transliteration mechanism. For handling foreign words, we used International-Phonetic-Alphabet(IPA)-based transliteration. Proposed system first tries to find if the word exists in English IPA diction-ary. If the word is not available in the English dictionary it uses the mechanism as proposed with Akkhor Bangla Software and a Bengali lexicon database to transliterate meaningful words. Our proposed approach improved the quality of Bangla transliteration input method by 14 points.

2 Related Works

There were several attempts in building Bengali transliteration systems. The first available free transliteration system from Bangladesh was Akkhor Bangla Software[1]. Akkhor was first released on 2003 which became very popular among computer users.

Zaman et. al. (2006) presented a phonetics based transliteration system for English to Bangla which produces intermediate code strings that facilitate matching pronunciations of input and desired output. They have used table-driven direct mapping techniques between the English alphabet and the Bangla alphabet, and a phonetic lexicon–enabled mapping. However they did not consider about transliterating foreign words. Most of the foreign words cannot be mapped using their mechanism.

Rahman et. al. (2007) compared different phonetic input methods for Bengali. Following Akkhor, many other software started offering Bengali transliteration. But none of these works considered about transliterating foreign words using IPA based approach.

Amitava Das et. Al. (2010) proposed a comprehensive transliteration method for Indic languages including Bengali. They also reported IPA based approach improved the performance for Bengali language.

3 Transliteration Architecture

In this paper, we propose a transliteration input method for Bangla language with special handling of foreign words. For transliterating we considered only English foreign words and simple rule-base mechanism. For foreign words, we used International-Phonetic-Alphabet (IPA) based transliteration.

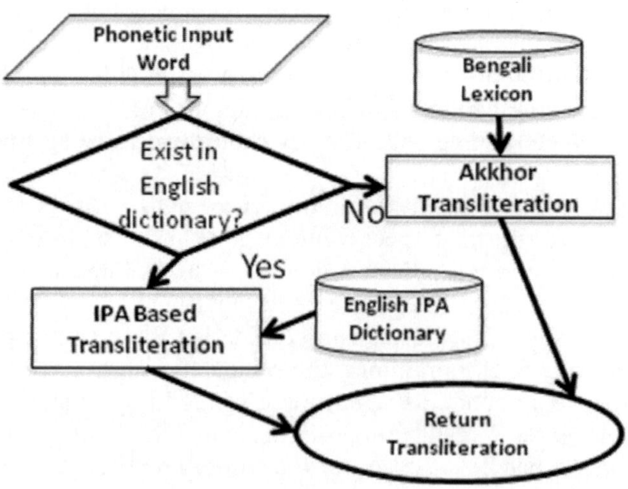

FIGURE 1. Proposed Transliteration Architecture

[1]http://www.akkhorbangla.com/

Figure 1 shows the Bengali transliteration process in a flow chart. Proposed system first tries to find if the word exists in English IPA dictionary to detect foreign words. For these foreign words, it uses IPA based transliteration. If the word is not available in the English dictionary, it uses Akkhor transliteration mechanism.

As Bengali language accepts many English foreign words, transliterating the English word into Bengali alphabet makes that a Bengali foreign word. In our assumption, when writing Bengali message people write English foreign words using English spelling. To identify such input words, the system first checks for a word for foreign (English) origin by looking up at the English IPA dictionary. If the word is not available in the English IPA dictionary, the system uses the transliteration mechanism as proposed with Akkhor Bangla Software and a Bengali lexicon database to transliterate Bengali words.

4 IPA Based Transliteration

From English IPA dictionary the system can obtain the English words pronunciations in IPA format. Output for this step is the Bengali word transliterated from the IPA of the English word. In this step, we use following English-Bengali Transliteration map to transliterate the IPA into Bengali alphabet.

Mouth narrower vertically	[i:] ই / ি sleep /sli:p/	[I] ই / ি slip /sl**I**p/	[ʊ] উ / ু book /bʊk/	[u:]ঊ/ ূ boot /bu:t/
	[e] এ / ে ten /ten/	[ə] আ / া after /a:ftə/	[ɜ:] আ / া bird /bɜ:d/	[ɔ:] র্ bored /bɔ:d/
Mouth wider vertically	[æ]এ্যা/ ্যা cat /kæt/	[^] **আ** / া cup / k^p/	[ɑ:] **আ** / া car / cɑ:r/	[ɒ] অ hot /hɒt/

Table 1. English-Bengali IPA chart for vowels

[**I**ə] ইয়া/িয়া beer /b**I**ər/	[e**I**] এই/ েই say /se**I**/	
[ʊə] উয়া/ ুয়া fewer /fjʊər/	[ɔ**I**] অয়/য় boy /bɔ**I**/	[ə ʊ] ও / ো no /nəʊ/
eə ঈয়া/ ীয়া bear /beər/	[a**I**] াই / আই high /ha**I**/	[aʊ]আউ / াউ cow /kaʊ/

Table 2. English-Bengali IPA chart for diphthongs

[p] প pan /pæn/	[b] ব ban /bæn/	[t] ট tan /tæn/	[d] ড day /deI/	[ʧ] চ chat /ʧæt/	[ʤ] জ judge /ʤ^ʤ/	[k] ক key /kiː/	[g] গ get /get/
[f] ফ fan /fæn/	[v] ভ van / væn/	[θ] থ thin /θIn/	[ð] দ than /ðæn/	[s] স sip /sIp/	[z] জ zip / zIp/	[ʃ] শ ship /ʃIp/	[ʒ] স vision /vIʒ^n/
[m] ম might /maIt/	[n] ন night /naIt/	[ŋ]ং/ঙ thing /θIŋ/	[h] হ height /haIt/	[l] ল light /laIt/	[r] র right /raIt/	[w] য় white /hwaIt/	[j]ইয়ে yes /jes/

Table 3. English-Bengali IPA chart for consonants

Table 1, 2 and 3 shows our proposed English-Bengali IPA chart for vowels, diphthongs and consonants. Using rule-base we transliterate the English IPA into Bangla alphabets. The above IPA charts leaves out many IPA as we are considering about translating from English only. To translate from other language such as Japanese to Banglawe need to create Japanese specific IPA transliteration chart. Using the above English-Bangla IPA chart we produced transliteration from the English IPA dictionary. For examples: pan(pæn): প্যান; ban(bæn): ব্যান; might(maIt): মাইট .

5 Akkhor Transliteration

বাংলা	অ	আ	ই	ঈ	উ	ঊ	ঋ	এ	ঐ	ও	ঔ
English	A	a/aa/`a	i/`i	I/ee/`I	u/`u	U/`U	ri/`ri	e/`e	oi/`oi	o/`o	ou ou

বাংলা	ক	খ	গ	ঘ	ঙ	চ	ছ	জ	ঝ	ঞ
English	k	kh	g	gh	Ng	ch	Ch	j	jh	Y
বাংলা	ত	থ	দ	ধ	ন	ট	ঠ	ড	ঢ	ণ
English	t	th	d	dh	n	T	Th	D	Dh	N
বাংলা	প	ফ	ব	ভ	ম	য	র	ল	শ	ষ
English	p	f/ph	b	bh/v	m	z	r	1	sh	S
বাংলা	গ	ক্ষ	হ	ড়	ঢ়	য়	ং	ঃ	ঁ	
English	S	k-S	h	R	rh	y	ng	:	~	
বাংলা	১	২	৩	৪	৫	৬	৭	৮	৯	০
English	1	2	3	4	5	6	7	8	9	1
বাংলা	কা	কে	কি	কু	কো	ক্র	ক্রে	ক্রি	ক্রু	ক্রূ
English	ka	ke	ki	ku	kO	kro	kre	kree	kru	krU
বাংলা	কী	চী	মী	কূ	মূ	বূ	ণূ	নূ	ক্য	ব্য
English	kI	chI	mI	kU	mU	bU	NU	nU	k-z	b-z

Table 4. Akkhor phonetic mapping for Bengali alphabets

Akkhor Bangla Software first implemented Bangla phonetic input method for computers. As a result this phonetic mapping become very popular among Bangladeshi computer users. However initially Akkhor did not consider about using Bangla Lexicon database. In this research we used Akkhor phonetic mapping with Bangla Lexicon database. Table 4 shows the phonetic mapping for Bengali alphabets.

Because of the ambiguities in mapping 50 Bengali letters using 26 English letters, any fixed Bengali Phonetic mapping is debatable. As a result different people have different assumptions on phonetic input system for Bengali language using English letters. To overcome this problem we used Bengali Lexicon which includes the IPA for each Bengali words. The system produces the Bengali transliteration by ranking the words using IPA string edit distance.

5.1 IPA String Edit Distance

IPA string edit distance assign a score to a sequence of acoustic observations X for a hypothesized string of phones P, but rely on different distributions for P (Droppo et. al. 2010). From these IPA string edit distance scores, we choose the highest scored transliteration and show the word candidates in descending order.

6 Experiment

Based on the above method we implemented the phonetic Bengali input method for computer and mobile devices. We evaluated the produced transliteration for our test-set including 200 words. This test-set mainly covered the foreign words from different domains. We have taken these words by averaging across multiple users' behaviour.

Table 5 shows our evaluation result, where we compared our proposed phonetic input method with the Akkhor Baseline. We manually checked the produced transliteration quality and assigned each test-set entry as wrong (W), correct (C) or neutral (N). Neutral refers to such words which can be correct in different context and it depends on the user intention. For example, ban can refer to both Bengali word বান and ব্যান. Therefore, we assign such ambiguous words as neutral or N. In our experiment, our proposed approach improved the quality of Bangla transliteration input method by 14 points. The proposed phonetic input method could correclt transliterate 68% of the test-set words.

Transliteration Quality	Akkhor Baseline	Proposed Phonetic Input Method
Correct (C)	54%	68%
Wrong (W)	39%	22%
Neutral (N)	7%	10%
Total	**100%**	**100%**

Table 5. Comparison between Akkhor transliteration and proposed phonetic input method

For example, Table 6 shows 3 sample transliterations produced by Akkhor Baseline and our proposed Phonetic Input Method. As we can see for first two examples Akkhor produced wrong (W) transliteration and our proposed phonetic input method produced correct (C) transliteration.

In third case, both are marked as neutral (N), because both words is correct in different context and it depends on the user intention.

#	Input	Akkhor Baseline	Proposed Phonetic Input Method
1.	School	সচুল (W)	স্কুল (C)
2.	University	উনিভেরসিতয় (W)	ইউনিভার্সিটি (C)
3.	ban	বান (N)	ব্যান (N)

Table 6. Sample Transliterations produced by Akkhor baseline and proposed method

7 Conclusion

We proposed a phonetic Bengali input method which is useful for computer and mobile devices by transliteration mechanism. Our proposed solution is effective especially for mobile devices due to low computational resources. For English foreign words, the system used International-Phonetic-Alphabet(IPA)-based transliteration method for Bangla language. Our proposed approach improved the quality of Bangla transliteration input method by 14 points. In future, this method can be expanded to consider about handling foreign words in other Indian languages.

References

Naushad UzZaman, Arnab Zaheen and Mumit Khan. A comprehensive roman (English)-to-Bengali transliteration scheme. Proceedings of International Conference on Computer Processing on Bangla. Dhaka, Bangladesh, 2006.

M. Ziaur Rahman and Foyzur Rahman. On the Context of Popular Input Methods and Analysis of Phonetic Schemes for Bengali Users., In Proceedings of the 10th International Conference on Computer & Information Technology, Jahangirnagar, Bangladesh, 2007.

Jasha Droppo and Alex Acero. Context Dependent Phonetic String Edit Distance for Automatic Speech Recognition, IEEE International Conference on Acoustics Speech and Signal Processing (ICASSP), Dallas, TX. 2010.

Amitava Das, Tanik Saikh, Tapabrata Mondal, Asif Ekbal, Sivaji Bandyopadhyay. English to Indian Languages Machine Transliteration System at NEWS 2010. Proceedings of the 2010 Named Entities Workshop, ACL 2010.

LuitPad: A fully Unicode compatible Assamese writing software

Navanath Saharia[1,3] *Kishori M Konwar*[2,3]
(1) Tezpur University, Tezpur, Assam, India
(2) University of British Columbia, Vancouver, Canada
(3) NavaPrabhat, Tezpur, Assam, India
navanathsaharia@gmail.com, kishori@engr.uconn.edu

ABSTRACT
LuitPad is a stand-alone, fully Unicode compliant software designed for rapid typing of Assamese words and characters. There are two main typing options; one which is based on approximate sound of words and the other based on the sound of characters, both of which are efficient and user-friendly, even for a first-time user. In addition, LuitPad comes with an online spell-checker; on "right-clock" over a misspelt word, presents the user with a list of relevant appropriate corrections for replacements. Assamese is an Indic language, spoken throughout North-Eastern parts of India by approximately 30 million people. There is a severe lack of user-friendly software available for typing Assamese text. This is perhaps the underlying reason for the miniscule presence of Assamese based information storage and retrieval systems, both off-line and on-line. With LuitPad, the user can retrieve Assamese characters and words using an English alphabet based keyboard in an effective and intuitive way. LuitPad is compatible with Windows, Mac and Linux with a GUI. The software can store the contents in LuitPad file format (".pad" extension) that can store images and text. In addition, .pad files can be easily exported to pdf and html files.

KEYWORDS: LuitPad, Assamese language, Unicode, text input.

*Corresponding author

1 Introduction

Assamese is one of the commonly spoken languages in the North-Eastern parts of India. Approximately 30 million people speak Assamese, and it is the regional official language in the state of Assam. Although Unicode points have been assigned for the Assamese alphabets Assamese texts on the Internet or in digitized format is almost non-existent. There are several hundred commonly used glyphs related to Assamese characters. At present, there is no text editing software to write Assamese texts in an effective manner. The most popular software, commonly used in desktop publishing shops and newspaper printing houses, is a non-Unicode based software. The software uses non-Unicode proprietary font files and reuses the ASCII code points to render non-English glyphs. In order to circumvent the limitation of just 127 ASCII codes, a set of segmented strokes are represented using ASCII codes in a font file. For example, in an ordinary font file the glyph at the hexadecimal code 0x41 is the shape for the letter "A" but in the custom designed font file it may look like something very different. Most of the characters are rendered by juxtaposing 2-3 of these strokes. In order to accommodate bold, italic and Assamese numerals there are other separate font files. Hence, an ASCII code can correspond to several different glyphs depending on the font file. As a result, typing characters involves pressing complex key combinations. This also confines inputting of Assamese texts on computers only to highly trained professionals. Due to the above mentioned difficulties and lack of effective Assamese text editing software Assamese text on the Internet, or any other digitized form, is very rare. Among the very few websites that use Assamese texts, mostly daily newspapers, the overwhelming majority presents their contents in the form of images of pages. This prohibits text searching and mining in Assamese documents.

LuitPad is developed to address the above difficulties of Assamese text editing on computers. It is designed to be able to edit Assamese text in Unicode by novice users with minimal effort and training. The Unicode complaint nature of LuitPad allows the user to copy Assamese text from the LuitPad editor to any email in the Unicode format, and view it elsewhere, with commonly used web-browsers (e.g. FireFox, Google Chrome, Internet Explorer, Safari, etc). In addition, approximate pronunciation based mode in the software prevents the user from making potential spelling mistakes by presenting a list of possible words. The interactively presented words are retrieved from an internal dictionary, with more than 60,000 Assamese words, which also includes proper nouns. Most Assamese dictionaries list about 30,000-40,000 words. The efficient retrieval of words is done by using elegant rapid searching data-structures and morphological trimming algorithms developed by the authors. In addition, the approximate pronunciation based search algorithms in LuitPad are tailored to commonly used Assamese.

The rest of the paper is organized as follows. In section 2 we describe previous work related to Assamese script and writing tools. Section 3 explains the features of LuitPad software; Section 4 discusses the experimental tests of the software; and finally, Section 5 concludes the paper.

2 Background on Assamese writing and previous work

Very few studies have been reported on the computational linguistic approaches of the Assamese language (Saharia et al., 2010, 2012; Sharma et al., 2002, 2008) and Assamese writing systems (Hinkle et al., 2010).

Brief description of the Assamese script Assamese writing has evolved from the ancient Indian script, *Brahmi.* Brahmi had various classes, and Assamese originated from Gupta Brahmi Script. The history of Assamese script and language can be divided into three main era, ancient, medieval and modern script. During each era, the language went though significant changes in terms of script, language and literature. The oldest Assamese inscriptions were found in the state of Assam are 5th century rock inscriptions at *Umachal* in *Guwahati*[1] and the *Nagajuri Khanikargaon inscription*, in Golaghat district. These two samples of inscription are in Sanskrit (Brahmi script). The *Kanai Barasi Bowa rock inscription* at *Rajaduar* in *north Guwahati*, dating back to 1205-06 AD, marks the first stage of evolution of the Assamese alphabet and deviation from Brahmi script. Assamese alphabets consist of 11 vowels, 41 consonants, 143-174 two-phoneme and 21-27 three-phoneme clusters of conjunct letters. Table 1 tabulates Assamese consonant and vowels and Table 2 shows digits, example of a consonant with example usage of vowel modifiers and a few instances of multiple cluster letters.

Consonants				
ক	খ	গ	ঘ	ঙ
চ	ছ	জ	ঝ	ঞ
ট	ঠ	ড	ঢ	ণ
ত	থ	দ	ধ	ন
প	ফ	ব	ভ	ম
য	ৰ	ল	ৱ	
শ	ষ	স	হ	
ক্ষ	ড়	ঢ়	য়	
ৎ	◌ং	◌ঃ	◌ঁ	

Vowels			
অ	আ	ই	ঈ
উ	ঊ	ঋ	
এ	ঐ	ও	ঔ

Table 1: Assamese consonants and vowels

Digits						
০	১	২	৩	৪	৫	৬
৭	৮	৯				

Consonant ক with vowel modifiers						
ক	কা	কি	কী	কু	কূ	কৃ
কে	কৈ	কো	কৌ			

Some two cluster letters						
ক্ক	ক্ল	ক্ত	ক্ম	ক্স	স্ম	প্ত
স্ক	ঙ্ক	স্ত	ঙ্গ	ন্ত	ত্ত	ন্ন
ল্ল	ষ্ণ	শু	হ্ল	স্ন	ষ্ট	প্প

Some three cluster letters					
ত্ত্ব	ন্ধ্র	স্ত্র	জ্জ্ব	ম্ব্র	ন্ধ্য

Table 2: Digits, consonants with vowel modifiers and, examples of 2 & 3 letter clusters.

Brief description of previously used techniques When we discuss text inputting software, usually the focus is on the soft-keyboards and other methods/techniques such as auto-completion, character/word prediction, handling morphology and word list etc. Due to the large (in the order of several hundreds) set of letters and conjunct letters (*cluster letters*), in comparison to the English alphabets, writing Assamese with an English keyboard is extremely inefficient, The Bureau of Indian Standards adopted ISCII[2] to represent text in Indian languages. After that, Unicode[3] adopted the ISCII with some modifications. Among the Indian languages Hindi, Bengali and Telugu are explored more

[1] The capital of the state of Assam and the gateway of North-Eastern India

[2] Indian Standard Code for Information Interchange (ISCII) is an 8-bit character encoding, for Indian languages originate from Brahmi script. ISCII is adopted as a standard by Bureau of Indian Standards (BIS) in 1991.

[3] An UNIversal enCODEing system, was initiated in January 1991, under the name Unicode, Inc., to promote a common encoding system to process text of all languages. Currently, Unicode is in version 6.1.0. It provides three different encoding formats: UTF-8, UTF-16 and UTF-32.

than other Indian languages. For soft-keyboards, only one Assamese specific work has been reported in (Hinkle et al., 2010). They proposed an efficient and adaptable soft keyboard for Assamese, using simple genetic algorithms. They also reported techniques for creating optimal language independent soft-keyboards. The product is not yet available in the market. Google(*iGoogle*) has a predictive soft-keyboard for Assamese. In this static keyboard, alphabets are arranged in the boundary of the input box. It has lesser number of keys since both the vowels and phonetic variant buttons are missing from the layout.

During our literature survey we found only a few tools available for Assamese text writing. Among them *Ramdhenu*[4], an ASCII based Windows tool is more popular in desktop printing businesses and new-papers. It is a hooking application that interfaces with the active application (for example MS Office, Notepad etc.) and change the font mapping to its own font *Geetanjali*. In the Geetanjali, the ASCII codes are assigned some carefully chosen strokes and segments in a way that the glyph for each character can be created by collating these segments. The main disadvantage of this tool is it is ASCII based, and difficult to input Assamese digits and cluster characters. It requires (*Ctrl* + *Shift*) key press combinations to input numerals. The user has to change font face in order to render italic or bold text. On the other hand, Avro (OmicronLab, 2012), Baraha (Baraha, 2012), Lipikaar (Lipikaar, 2012) and Sabdalipii (Sabdalipi, 2012) are Unicode based writing tools, the first three are for all Indian languages and final one is specifically for Assamese. Avro and Baraha supports phonetics based writing but requires quite a large number of key strokes. Baraha, Sabdalipi and Lipikaar have integrated text editors. Google and Wikipedia have developed soft keyboards for Brahmic scripts, but these are not optimized(Hinkle et al., 2010), and therefore, inefficient to use.

3 Description of LuitPad

LuitPad is designed to make inputting of Assamese text efficient in the Unicode format, by lay users and professional typists. LuitPad achieves this by allowing the user to retrieve Assamese characters and words, with English alphabet based keyboards, in an effective and intuitive way. This helps the user to use LuitPad effectively, with less than 20 minutes of training. In addition, it prevents the user from making potential spelling mistakes by utilizing an internal dictionary of more than 60,000 Assamese words including proper nouns. In the remainder of the article, by "character" we mean Assamese characters and when we refer to English or Roman alphabets we do so explicitly. All the keys and keyboards we refer to are based on the Roman or English alphabet. Following are the fundamental features of LuitPad that are pertinent to text inputting.

1. LuitPad has two primary modes of input: *character* mode, where characters are entered one at a time; and the *word* mode, where user can input Assamese words by typing an "approximate" phoneme of the Assamese word, in Roman alphabets.

2. In the character mode, each Assamese alphabet is mapped from a prefix string of Roman alphabets (usually, 1-3 characters long). The mapping is customizable by the user to suit her preferred way of pronouncing Assamese characters, using Roman alphabets. Multiple users can store, retrieve and change their mapping in their personalized profiles, in the same installation of LuitPad.

[4]Ramdhenu Inc.

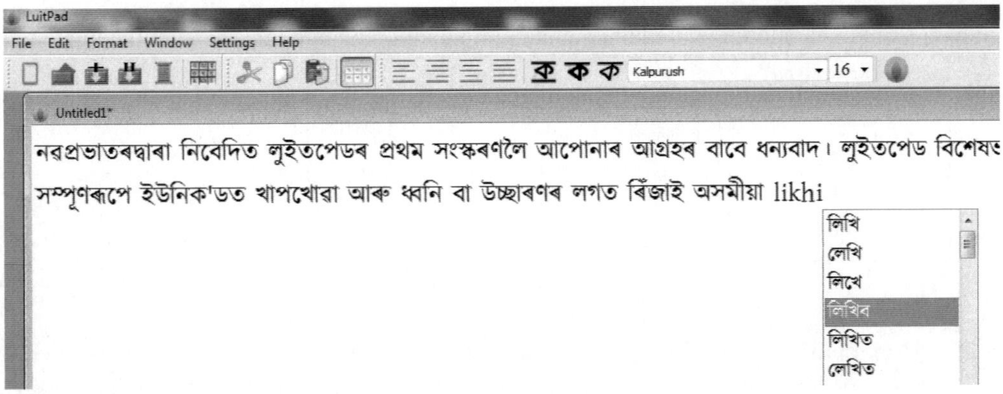

Figure 1: The front end GUI of LuitPad, in the Windows version, with a editor window showing a few lines of Assamese text and an image.

3. In the character mode, most of the Assamese words can be retrieved on the text editor by just typing the first few characters and pressing the *Ctrl* key. This brings up a list of words from an internal built-in Assamese dictionary. Apart from not having to type the entire word, this also reduces the possibility of making spelling mistakes.

4. LuitPad is also equipped with a spell checker for Assamese words and prompts a list of relevant corrections for spelling mistakes.

5. LuitPad text editor allows inserting, positioning and resizing of images.

6. Documents edited using LuitPad can be saved as a .pad file; and also can be edited later using LuitPad. The .pad file format is designed specifically for LuitPad.

7. Files created with the LuitPad text editor can be saved in PDF and HTML format for printing or other official works.

8. New words can be added to the built-in dictionary, while writing, simply by right clicking the mouse and choosing the "Add to dictionary" option; and similarly, already added words can be deleted by using the "Delete from dictionary". The added words can also be recalled using the *Ctrl* key as described above.

9. Any document written in the Geetanjali (a popular non-Unicode format for Assamese) font can be seamlessly converted to and fro to Unicode format by copy/paste.

10. LuitPad is a stand software, 100% Unicode compliant, and runs on Windows, Linux and Mac computers.

3.1 Input modes in more detail

LuitPad has the text input modes: *character* and *word* modes. The selected texts are always entered at the cursor. Below we describe these two modes in more detail.

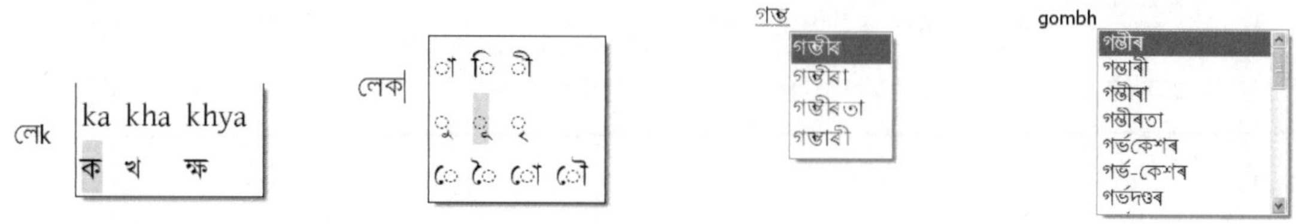

(a) (b) (c) (d)

Figure 2: (a) In character mode a pop-up presents the set of possible characters to choose from. (b) A vowel modifier list pop-ups, if the "Automatic Matra" option is turned on, in the character mode after non-vowel character. (c) Prefix based recalling of dictionary words in character mode. (d) In word mode, recalling dictionary words with approximate pronunciation in Roman alphabets.

Character mode: In this mode, each character in the Assamese alphabet, just consonants, vowels and vowel modifiers but not conjuncts, is mapped to a short string of Roman alphabets (usually, 1-4 characters but there is no length limit and they are customizable by the user). For example, the characters ক, খ and ক্ষ are mapped by *ka*, *kha* and *khya*, respectively. The digits 0-9 on the keyboard are mapped to the corresponding Assamese digits. When a user types any prefix of the mapped strings, in Roman alphabets, all the corresponding Assamese characters are presented on a tool-tip pop-up window, for the user to choose from. The *left* (←) and *right* (→) keys can be used, followed by <Enter>, to choose the desired character. The chosen character is inserted into the text editor. For example, consider the mapping, mentioned above, for the characters ক, খ and ক্ষ and suppose these are the only characters that have mapped strings beginning with the Roman alphabet "k". Upon typing "k" the the tool-tip window shows ক, খ and ক্ষ If "h" is pressed next, the characters খ and ক্ষ corresponding to the prefixes "kha" and "khya" will appear in the tool-tip window. Therefore, as the user progressively types out a possible mapped prefix the choices get narrower. If the user types out a possible mapping string which is not mapped to any character then the tool-tip window stops appearing. If "Automatic Character Fill" option, under the "Settings" menu is on and the prefix corresponds to only one possible character, then the character is automatically inserted, without requiring the <Enter> key-press. In addition, if the "Automatic Matra" option, in the "Settings" menu, is on and if the entered character is a consonant, a tool-tip window with the possible vowel modifiers is shown. If the user does not want to select a vowel modifier, she can continue entering the next character. In order to reduce typing, an entire word can be retrieved by typing the first few characters followed by a *Ctrl* key press. This will bring up a drop down list of words containing the prefix to choose from. Conjuncts can be created by pressing <Escape>, with the cursor at the end of a juxtaposition of the consonants.

Word mode: In the *word mode* entire Assamese words can be inserted just by typing an approximate phoneme for the Assamese word. The "approximate" phoneme helps accommodate different phonetic sounds for the same word, by different users. For example, the phonemes "karma", "korma", "kormo" and "karmo" might be used by different users to retrieve same word কর্ম. A dynamically changing drop down list helps the user to navigate to

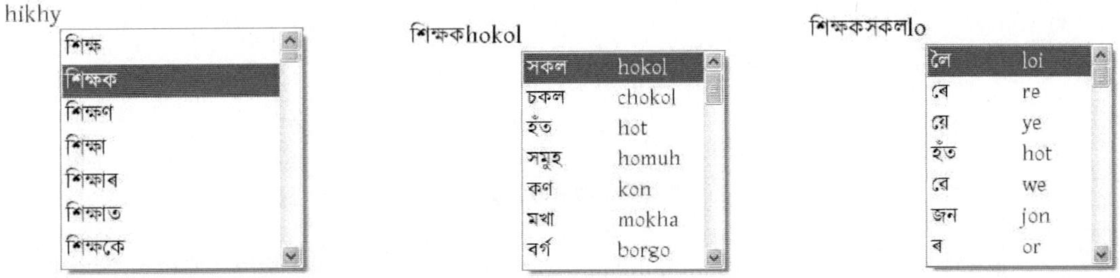

(a) (b) (c)

Figure 3: The stages of typing a word with morphological inflections. (a) Root word, (b) first inflection and (c) second inflection

the correct word, to deal with possible ambiguity. The list is updated with the completion of each key stroke. Once the user selects a word from the list, using the up(↑)/down(↓) keys, the selected word is inserted at the cursor. After the user enters a word then if the user presses <Space> bar then the process of inserting a separate word starts. However, if the user continues typing, without pressing <Space> bar, then the key strokes are interpreted to a get list of closest matching morphological inflections. It is worth mentioning here that Assamese is a highly inflectional language, and a root word may have up to 1500 inflectional forms. Consider the word শিক্ষকসকললৈ which can be broken into the root word, followed by morphological inflections as, শিক্ষকসকললৈ → শিক্ষক (root word) + সকল (inflection) + লৈ (inflection). The sequence of selections leading to the entering of the entire word শিক্ষকসকললৈ is shown in Figure 3. In practice, we observed a substantial improvement in the efficiency of Assamese text typing by common users. The users could type up to 15-20 words per minute in LuitPad as opposed to 5-8 words per minute using other available software.

Spell checker LuitPad has a spell checker for Assamese words. Based on its internal dictionary the words with incorrect spellings are flagged with a red under line. The user can choose to ignore any spelling error marks by clicking the ignore tab. The list of words, deemed spelling errors, are ignored in the document and does not affect other documents. This ignore list is stored as a part of the data-structure of the ".pad" file. However, in order to add a word to the ignore list to all documents the the unrecognized word should be added to the dictionary. The basic mechanism of the spell checking feature is done by computing the Levenshtein distance between a word and the words in the dictionary. Note this pairwise distance computation can introduce a perceptible delay in the distance computation. Therefore, we have created an algorithm and a data-structure that avoids such pair wise but rather does a directed search in the dictionary. Although, a morphologically inflected form of a word may not be in the dictionary we use a stemming algorithm to compute the list of root words, at most 4-5, to do the search.

3.2 Algorithms and data curation

The most commonly used algorithms, in the software, are various forms of basic tree based algorithms commonly presented in any data-structure text book. The Levenshtein distance,

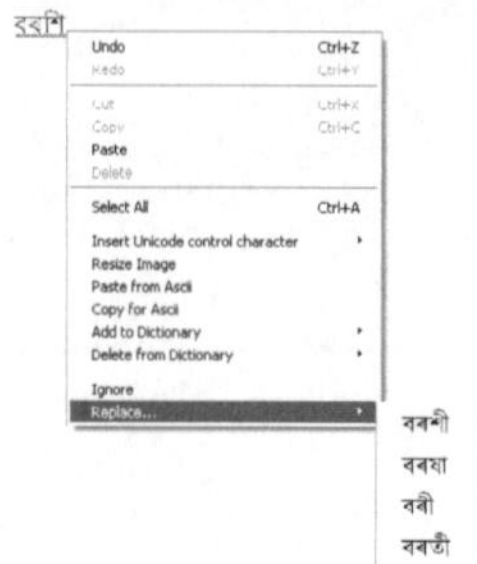

Figure 4: The LuitPad spell checker, with its presented correct choices, for a misspelt word. In the above case the top choice is the correct choice. The figure shows only the top five choices.

between two words, calculations are done using dynamic programming algorithms, implementation by the authors. The penalty matrix for the distance computation algorithms are based on linguistic proximity of the characters. For example, two similar sounding vowels are assigned a lower penalty value. The internal dictionary used, in its current form is only a list of Assamese words. Some of the words are with morphological inflections. The list of words are collected for a variety of sources, such as online dictionaries, bloggins sites. The gathered words are first programatically filtered for basic inconsistencies and later curated one by one. At its current state there are slightly more than 75,000 entries in the dictionary.

4 Experiments with users

Since its inception, LuitPad has been designed, and often redesigned, based on the feedback from various users. Some features were added based on the average users' preferences and others were deleted. We also conducted a quantitative test on the software. The authors are not aware of any benchmarking text dataset, designed for evaluation of typing speed, for the Assamese language. We evaluated the words per minute typing speed, for a group of 14 users by letting them type from commonly printed text. Half of the users do not write Assamese text language on a regular basis, but they can read very well The mean reciprocal rank(MRR), for the retrieval of list of words in the phonetic mode, is computed as the average of the reciprocals of 100 word searches from a popular magazine. Words that did not show up in among the, mostly proper nouns, were ranked infinity, the reciprocal of which is taken as zero. The accuracy of the spell checker is computed based on the percentage of appearance of the correctly spelt word, among the list of suggestions (a maximum of 10 suggestions are presented by the software).

#Users	Words per min	Spell checker accuracy	MRR
14	8-22	93%	0.76

Table 3: Results of the experiments on accuracy and speed of LuitPad.

5 Conclusion

In this paper we described a software, LuitPad, developed for Assamese text writing, in an efficient way. Future work will involve including it to other Indic languages, such as, Oriya, Bengali, Manipuri, Hindi, Marathi, etc. This because these languages have a similar origin and overlapping features in terms of character, conjuncts and vowel modifiers. In most of the cases in order to support one of the above Indian languages, the major changes would be to update the list of Unicodes for their glyphs, phonetic sound of alphabets and a reasonable dictionary. In addition, the internal parameters of the search algorithms used will be calibrated automatically to the user.

Acknowledgments

The authors would like to thank the anonymous reviewers for their valuable feedback and suggestions for improvements. The authors would like thank Maura Hickey for her critical suggestions on the overall content of the paper. Finally, they would like to thank Lovleena Konwar, Sudipto Konwar, Jahnobi Konwar, Dharitri Borgohain and Jyoti Konwar for curating the internal dictionary and testing the software; and Thapelo Vundhla for perusing the final version of the draft and making valuable suggestions.

References

Baraha (2012). Accessed: 2/10/2012.
URL `http://www.baraha.com`

Hinkle, L., Lezcano, M., & Kalita, J. (2010). Designing soft keyboards for Brahmic scripts. In *Proceedings of 8th International Conference on Natural Language Processing*. India: Macmillan Publishers.

Lipikaar (2012). Accessed: 2/10/2012.
URL `http://www.lipikaar.com`

OmicronLab (2012). Accessed: 2/10/2012.
URL `http://www.omicronlab.com`

Sabdalipi (2012). Accessed: 2/10/2012.
URL `http://www.tiassam.com/sabdalipi`

Saharia, N., Sharma, U., & Kalita, J. (2010). A suffix-based noun and verb classifier for an inflectional language. In *Proceedings of the 2010 International Conference on Asian Language Processing*, IALP '10, (pp. 19–22). Washington, DC, USA: IEEE Computer Society.
URL `http://dx.doi.org/10.1109/IALP.2010.64`

Saharia, N., Sharma, U., & Kalita, J. (2012). Analysis and evaluation of stemming algorithms: a case study with Assamese. In *Proceedings of the International Conference on Advances in Computing, Communications and Informatics*, ICACCI '12, (pp. 842–846). New York, NY, USA: ACM.
URL `http://doi.acm.org/10.1145/2345396.2345533`

Sharma, U., Kalita, J., & Das, R. (2002). Unsupervised learning of morphology for building lexicon for a highly inflectional language. In *Proceedings of the ACL-02 workshop on Morphological and phonological learning*.

Sharma, U., Kalita, J. K., & Das, R. K. (2008). Acquisition of morphology of an indic language from text corpus. *ACM Transactions of Asian Language Information Processing (TALIP)*, *7*(3), 9:1–9:33.
URL `http://doi.acm.org/10.1145/1386869.1386871`

Romanized Arabic Transliteration

Achraf Chalabi[1] *Hany Gerges*[2]
(1) Microsoft Research, Advanced Technology Lab, Cairo
(2) Microsoft Corp, One Microsoft Way, Redmond, WA, 98052

achalabi@microsoft.com, hanyg@microsoft.com

ABSTRACT

In the early 1990's, online communication was restricted to ASCII (English) only environments. A convention evolved for typing Arabic in Roman characters, this scripting took various names including: Franco Arabic, Romanized Arabic, Arabizi, Arabish, etc... The convention was widely adopted and today, romanized Arabic (RAr) is everywhere: In instant messaging, forums, blog postings, product and movie ads, on mobile phones and on TV! The problem is that the majority of Arab users are more used to the English keyboard layout, and while romanized Arabic is easier to type, Arabic is significantly easier to read, the obvious solution was automatic conversion of romanized Arabic to Arabic script, which would also lead to increasing the amount and quality of authored Arabic online content. The main challenges are that no standard convention of Romanized Arabic (many → 1 mappings) is available and there are no parallel data available. We present here a hybrid approach that we devised and implemented to build a romanized Arabic transliteration engine that was later on scaled to cover other scripts. Our approach leverages the work done by Sherif and Kondrak's (2007b) and Cherry and Suzuki (2009), and is heavily inspired by the basic phrase-based statistical machine translation approach devised by (Och, 2003).

KEYWORDS : Transliteration, Romanized Arabic, Franco-Arab, Maren, Arabic IME

1 Introduction

Transliteration automates the conversion from a source text into the corresponding target text, where usually both source and target texts are written suing different scripts. Both texts might belong to the same language as in the case of "Roman-script Arabic" to "Arabic-script Arabic" or to two different languages as in the case where the source text is English written in Roman script and the target one is Arabic written in Arabic script.

Our initial implementation was targeting the transliteration of colloquial Arabic, written in roman script, into colloquial Arabic written in Arabic script. Later on the same engine has been used to transliterate English text written in roman characters into Arabic written in Arabic script and visa-versa, then it was scaled to cover other scripts such as Farsi, Hebrew, Urdu and many others.

The engine was integrated into a multitude of applications, the first one being a TSF (Text Service Framework) component. TSF provides a simple and scalable framework for the delivery of advanced text input and natural language technologies. It can be enabled in applications, or as a text service. TSF services provide multilingual support and deliver text services such as keyboard processors, handwriting recognition, and speech recognition.

In this design, TSF was used to provide a candidate list for what the user types-in across Windows applications, and the service is easily discoverable through the language bar. The user will be able to get the transliteration functionality in any TSF-Aware control (e.g. RichEdit).

The second target application is Machine Translation, where transliteration will be called to address out-of-vocabulary words, mostly named entities.

Having the above target applications in mind, the design should be devised in a way to account for all relevant requirements and expectations in terms of scalability, accuracy, functionality, robustness and performance.

The first section of this paper presents the architecture that we devised to implement our transliteration engine initially targeting romanized Arabic conversion. In the second section, we present an innovative technique for extracting training data out of parallel sentences, for training a "named entity" transliterator. In the third section we present our scoring mechanism, and in section 4, we present our evaluation and results.

2 Challenges

One of the key challenges we faced was to collect data to build the colloquial Arabic corpus. The biggest portion of this data was generated through the "Blog Muncher", an in-house crawling tool that scraps predefined public blog sites on a regular basis.

Figure 1 below shows a breakdown of the different sources and sizes of the data we were able to collect:

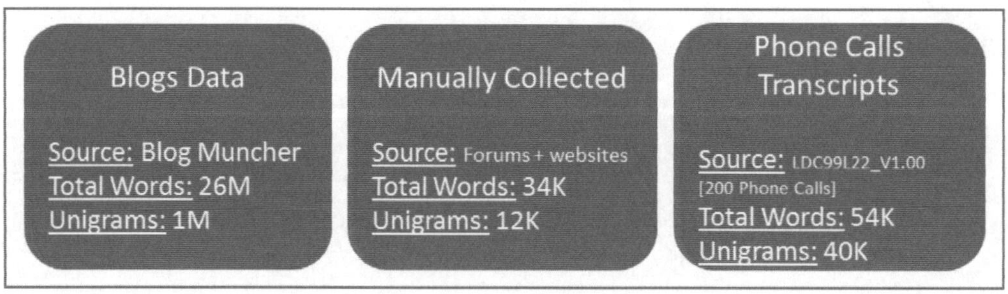

FIGURE 1 – Sources of the colloquial Arabic corpus.

Another challenge was the collection of parallel romanized Arabic data. We had to build this parallel data manually, using the vocabulary of the monolingual RAr corpus, amounting 35K words and had them human-translated. And while the monolingual corpus was used to train the target language models, the parallel data was used to train the transliteration model.

3 Architecture

3.1 Design Criteria

The design of the transliteration engine fulfills the following major criteria:

- Independent of the language-pair processed so that the same engine would process different language pairs.
- Independent of the calling application, where the initial applications under consideration are: Text Windows service, Machine Translation and on-line transliteration.
- Independent of the way the different models have been generated. Currently both rule-based and alignment-based transliterations are considered.
- Supports integration with C++, C# Applications and ASP pages
- Supports remote calls through the cloud, Web Services.
- The candidates should be ranked in context.
- Response time should be real-time.

3.2 Design

Our Transliteration architecture is based on a hybrid approach that combines both rule-based techniques and SMT-like techniques, as shown in Figure 2, consisting of the following modules:

- *Candidate Generator:* The module that will generate all possible candidates based on the Translation Model
- *Scorer/Ranker:* The module that computes scores for candidates based on different models.
- *Translation Model:* The data object carrying the possible segment mappings between source and target along with the corresponding probabilities.
- *Word Language Model:* Target Language Model carrying probabilities of word unigrams, extensible to bigrams and trigrams probabilities in later versions.
- *Character Language Model:* Target Language Model carrying probabilities of characters unigrams, bigrams and trigrams.
- *Configuration data:* The configuration data file specifying language pair-specific information including the location of related data models.
- *Transliteration Workbench:* The application developed in-house to generate various language models, used also to test and evaluate the engine.

The transliteration process is done in 2 phases. In the first phase, the candidate generator module generates all possible hypotheses. It is driven by the transliteration model which is composed of the mapping rules, and their probabilities. The rules could be either (i) handcrafted by a linguist through a rules editor, assisted by the source language corpus. In that case the rules probabilities are learned through a parallel corpus, or (ii) if the training data is big enough, the transliteration model could be learned automatically through automatic alignment.

In the second phase, the generated hypotheses are scored and ranked based on a log-linear combination of 3 different models: the original transliteration model, the target language word model, and the character-level model. Both target language models are generated using MSR LM toolkit, trained through the target language corpus.

The system parameters are tuned for Mean Reciprocal Ranking score, using the evaluator. The individual tools were integrated in a pipeline environment that we called "Transliterator Workbench".

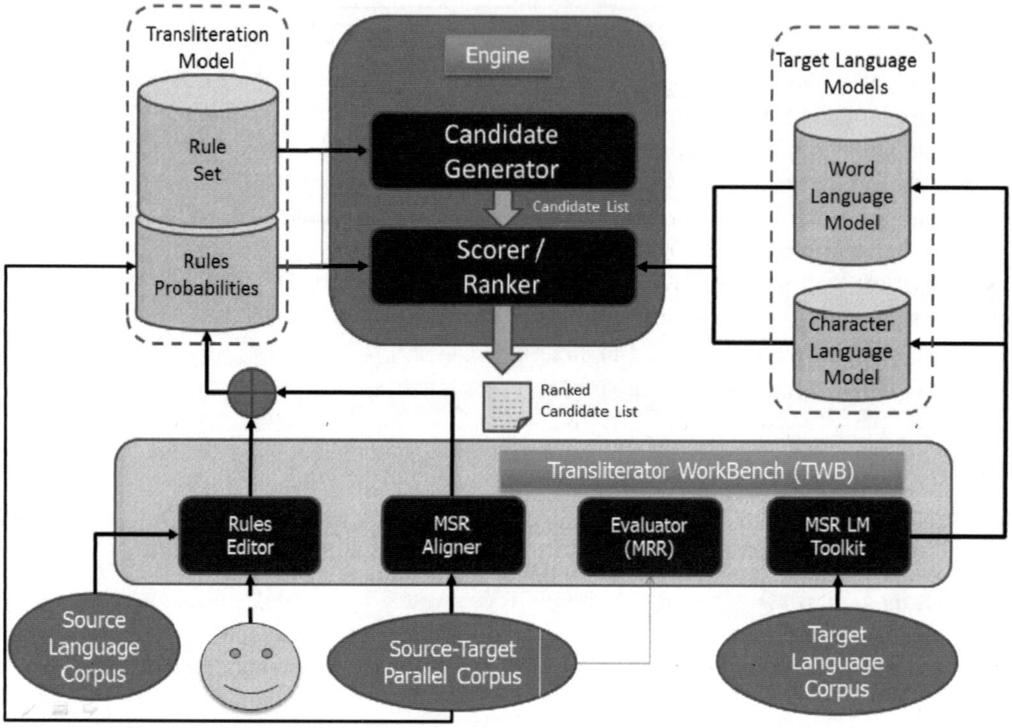

FIGURE 2 – Hybrid architecture of the transliteration engine.

3.3 Pruning Candidate paths

In order to optimize speed and space, pruning the candidates is crucial. In our approach, we applied pruning at each character position while dynamically computing incremental score based on both the transliteration model and character models. We then computed the accuracy loss in coordination with the pruning factor, and selected the default pruning factor as the one that would account for an accuracy loss <= 1% of the best produced accuracy.

To guarantee real-time response in the worst case scenario, we have set a predefined time limit for triggering aggressive pruning that is also dependent of the target task. We dynamically increase pruning when predefined time limit has been reached at different character positions, till first-best.

As shown in Figure 3 below, initial pruning results show a loss of 0.1% in accuracy at 100-best, with a translation table (rule set) of 1300 entries. Where Acc-BF is the accuracy using Breadth-first strategy, Acc-DF is the accuracy using Depth-first strategy, and MRR is the mean reciprocal rank accuracy.

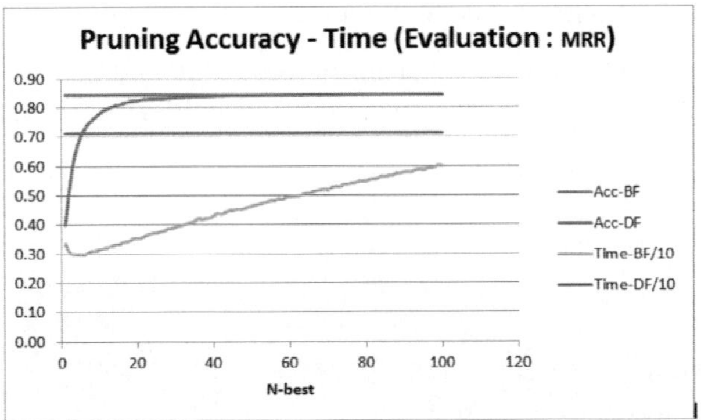

FIGURE 3 –MRR Accuracy vs. pruning thresholds.

3.4 Stemming

In many cases, especially with long input strings, the required performance could not be met, so we resorted to stemming the input strings. This would improve performance, and increase recall to account for such cases where all generated hypotheses were not found in the language model, and where the input word contains potential affixes. The affixes list is predefined with their corresponding transliterations.

Whenever the stripping of a given suffix, prefix or prefix-suffix combination leads to candidates seen in the target LM, the affixes' transliterations are concatenated to the generated candidates.

There are 2 strategies to be considered here:

1. Exhaust all possible affixes.
2. Exit on first success, in which case the affixes lists need to be prioritized.

Both strategies have been experimented, and decision was made based on the accuracy/speed results. We also used large enough dictionary (10K+) which enabled us to stem the input word and match it against the dictionary prior to calling the candidate generator, and resulted in a sensible impact on the system performance.

4 Scoring

Ranking the generated hypotheses is based on the individual candidates' score. Inspired by the linear models used in SMT (Och,2003), we can discriminatively weight the components of the generative model, and compute each candidate score based on a weighted log-linear combination of 3 models, as per the formula below:

$$\lambda_T \log P_T(s|t) + \lambda_C \log P_C(t) + \lambda_W \log P_W(t)$$

Where emission information is provided by $P_T(s|t)$, estimated by maximum likelihood on the operations observed in our training derivations. $P_C(t)$ provides transition information through a target character language model, estimated on the target corpus. In our implementation, we use a

KN-smoothed trigram model (Kneser and Ney, 1995). $P_W(t)$ is a unigram target word model, estimated from the same target corpus used to build our character language model.

Since each model's contribution is different than the other, we need to estimate weights values (λ_T, λ_C, λ_W) that would maximize system's accuracy. We used 10% of the parallel data for λ-training, and isolated another 10% as a test set.

5 Evaluation

We have adopted two evaluation metrics, namely the mean reciprocal rank (MRR) and Topmost candidate, both techniques are on the word-level:

Mean reciprocal rank is a measure for evaluating any process that produces a list of possible responses to an input, ordered by probability of correctness. The reciprocal rank of a given input is the multiplicative inverse of the rank of the first correct answer. The mean reciprocal rank is the average of the reciprocal ranks of results for a sample of input strings.

In the Topmost technique, only the first (topmost) candidate, i.e the one with the highest probability of correctness is considered during evaluation. The evaluation is done on the word-level, by comparing the generated candidate with the reference.

- To account for applications where no further selection could be allowed, the Top candidates only were evaluated against the gold standard.
- And for other applications where further selection was allowed, we evaluate the MRR for the n-best candidates, in our case, we considered the 5-best candidates:
    - Linear scoring: assign $(1-i)/n$ for the ith candidate in an n-best scheme
    - MRR : assign $1/(i+1)$ for the ith candidate in an n-best scheme

Metric	Value
Top Candidate Ratio	85 %
Linear Scoring	95%
MRR	90%

TABLE 1 – Evaluation Results for the RAr transliterator

Table 1 above shows the results of the hybrid system for the different metrics using a test set of 5K words. We were able to achieve 90% accuracy on the MRR metric considering the 5-best candidates, and 85% considering only the top candidate only.

6 Scaling to Other Languages

To overcome the lack of training data, we have used a generative model constrained with the target language to extract parallel named entities out of parallel sentences, as depicted in the diagram shown in Figure 4 below:

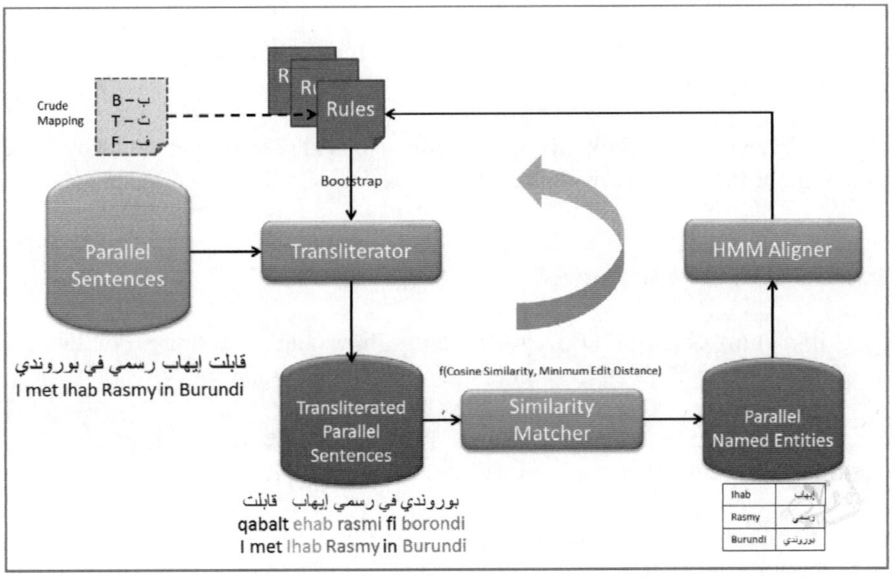

FIGURE 4 –Extraction of Parallel NE from Parallel sentences.

Starting with a very crude mapping of letters, we can build an initial shallow set of rules, and use it to bootstrap a primitive transliterator.

Then using that shallow transliterator and a corpus of parallel sentences, used to train Machine Translation, we transliterate the source sentences. Leveraging the fact that the transliteration of proper names is usually very similar, if not equal, to its translation, we use similarity matching, based on a combination of minimum edit distance and cosine similarity, to spot corresponding named entities in both the source and target sentences and come up with a list of parallel Names. Then using monotonic alignment, we can augment the rule set in an iterative way.

Using this methodology, we were able to scale our transliteration framework to other languages and develop both the Hebrew-to-English and the Farsi-to-English transliterators.

Conclusion

The hybrid architecture proved to be quite efficient, since for those languages where human expertise was available, and the amount of parallel training data was very little, the number of segment alignments was relatively tiny as compared to the size learned from parallel data, resulting in an increased performance. On the other hand, whenever human expertise was absent, and enough training data was available, the framework was still able to produce models for other languages and scripts. Leveraging the generative model to extract parallel Named Entities out of parallel sentences has opened new doors enabling easy scalability to many other languages, especially those for which MT parallel training data is available.

References

Yaser Al-Onaizan and Kevin Knight. 2002. Machine transliteration of names in Arabic text. In *ACL Workshop on Comp. Approaches to Semitic Languages*.

Shane Bergsma and Grzegorz Kondrak. 2007. Alignment-based discriminative string similarity. In *ACL*, pages 656–663, Prague, Czech Republic, June.

Slaven Bilac and Hozumi Tanaka. 2004. A hybrid back-transliteration system for Japanese. In *COLING*, pages 597–603, Geneva, Switzerland.

Dayne Freitag and Shahram Khadivi. 2007. A sequence alignment model based on the averaged perceptron. In *EMNLP*, pages 238–247, Prague, Czech Republic, June.

Ulf Hermjakob, Kevin Knight, and Hal Daum´e III. 2008. Name translation in statistical machine translation - learning when to transliterate. In *ACL*, pages 389–397, Columbus, Ohio, June.

Sittichai Jiampojamarn, Colin Cherry, and Grzegorz Kondrak. 2008. Joint processing and discriminative training for letter-to-phoneme conversion. In *ACL*, pages 905–913, Columbus, Ohio, June.

Kevin Knight and Jonathan Graehl. 1998. Machine transliteration. *Computational Linguistics*, 24(4):599–612.

Colin Cherry and Hisami Suzuki. 2009. Discriminative Substring Decoding for Transliteration, In EMNLP.

Philipp Koehn, Franz J. Och, and Daniel Marcu. 2003. Statistical phrase-based translation. In *HLT-NAACL*.

Haizhou Li, Min Zhang, and Jian Su. 2004. A joint source-channel model for machine transliteration. In *ACL*, pages 159–166, Barcelona, Spain, July.

Eric Sven Ristad and Peter N. Yianilos. 1998. Learning string-edit distance. *IEEE Transactions on Pattern Analysis and Machine Intelligence*, 20(5):522–532.

Tarek Sherif and Grzegorz Kondrak. 2007b. Substring-based transliteration. In *ACL*, pages 944–951, Prague, Czech Republic, June.

Reinhard Kneser and Hermann Ney. 1995. Improved backing-off for m-gram language modeling. In *International Conference on Acoustics, Speech, and Signal Processing (ICASSP-95)*, pages 181–184.

Forward Transliteration of Dzongkha Text to Braille

TirthankarDasgupta Manjira Sinha Anupam Basu
Indian Institute of Technology Kharagpur
{iamtirthankar, manjira87, anupambas}@gmail.com

ABSTRACT

In this paper we present an automatic Dzongkha text to Braille forward transliteration system. Dzongkha is the national language of Bhutan. The system is aimed at providing low cost efficient access mechanisms for blind people. It also addresses the problem of scarcity of having automatic Braille transliteration systems in language slime Dzongkha. The present system can be configured to take Dzongkha text document as input and based on some transliteration rules it generates the corresponding Braille output. We further extended the system to support an Audio QWERTY editor which allows a blind person to read and write Dzongkha texts or its equivalent Braille through a computer. The editor also contains Dzongkha voice feedbacks to further ease the use.

KEYWORDS: Braille, Forward Transliteration, Dzongkha, Audio QWERTY

1 Introduction

The Braille encoding system is one of the primary means of representing textual documents in a readable format for the Blind persons (Loaber, 1976; Weller and Klema, 1965; Basu et al,, 1998; Lahiri et al., 2005). However, due to the scarcity of Braille compatible reading materials, blind people face difficulty in fulfilling necessities like education and employment. The unavailability of low-cost technical supports worsens the situation further. For them, the inability to communicate via the traditional writing system leads to complications at official places where the primary mode is still through writing. In order to bridge between the written text systems generally aimed at sighted persons and access mechanisms through which blind people can communicate with ease and efficiency, developments of systems such as automatic Braille transliteration and screen readers are highly needed.

Several works have been done on building automatic, bi-directional text to Braille transliteration system and speech enabled interfaces for the Blind community (Blenkhorn, 1995; Pennington and McCoy, 1998; Raman, 1996). However, all the present systems suffer from the central limitation of language dependency. A Braille transliteration system requires certain rules, based on which the system automatically transliterate a given text document into Braille. The rules are very specific to the input language. Therefore, system for a particular language cannot be extended to the others.

Dzongkha is the national language of Bhutan[1]. It has been found that more than 4% of the children in Bhutan suffer from early blindness. Therefore, it is essential to develop tools and technologies in such a country that will facilitate blind persons to access information from written text documents. The existing text on Braille transliteration systems cannot be directly applied to Dzongkha, mainly due to the following reasons:

1. Most of the systems are based on foreign languages like English, French, Germany, Spanish, Portuguese, and Swedish (winbraille, 2012; Duxbury, 2000; indexbraille, 2012; NFBTRANS, 2004). As Bhutanese scripts are quite different from these languages, separate rules are applied to transliterate from Dzongkha to Braille.
2. Foreign systems like, Duxbury (2004) and JAWS (2008) are costly and a large segment of the blind population is from poor economic background.

In order to overcome the limitations of the existing systems, we have developed a Dzongkha language text to Braille transliteration (DLBT) system. The system comprises of the following two key features:

i. A generic framework for the transliteration of Dzongkha texts to Braille.

ii. An audio QWERTY editor that provides pre-recorded voice feedback to any key-press operation performed by a blind user.

Apart from creating Braille encoded textbooks, such system will also assist blind people to create their own electronic text documents.

The rest of the paper is organized as follows: section 2 briefly discusses about the state of the art in text to Braille transliteration systems; in section 3 we have discussed about the Dzongkha

---

[1] http://en.wikipedia.org/wiki/Languages_of_Bhutan

Braille encoding system; in section 4 we have described the architecture of our proposed system and its the key components; we have discussed the Audio QWERTY editor in section 5 and finally concluded the paper in section 6.

2 Related Works

A number of texts to Braille transliteration tools are present for different languages. In English, systems like, Duxbury (2000), JAWS (2008), and WinBraille (2012) are popularly used. However, the problem of transliterating English text to Braille is relatively simpler than south-east Asian languages like, Indian or Bhutanese languages. It has been observed that due to the similarity in the scripts of these languages, rules to transliterate Dzongkha texts to Braille are very similar to that of the Indian language texts. The Sparsha Text to Braille Transliteration toolset (Lahiri et al., 2005; Dasgupta and Basu, 2009) is the only system encountered by us so far that can transliterate Indian language texts to Braille. The system provides some unique features like transliteration of mathematical symbols and tactile graphics to Braille. Apart from computer based transliterations of Braille, a Braille writing tutor system has been developed by Kalra et al. (2007). The prototype tutor system uses an e-slate device to capture a student's action and tries to develop the Braille writing skills.

3 The Dzongkha Braille Encoding System

The Dzongkha Braille system is the standard technique of representing Dzongkha texts into Braille (Tibetan, 2004; Dzongkha, 2005). The system uses 6 dot cells to represent each Dzongkha character. The combination of these 6 dots can represent a total of 2^6-1 i.e., 63 different Braille characters. However, as described later, Dzongkha has more than 63 characters. This issue is handled by assigning multiple Braille characters for a single source language character. This is illustrated in the third row of table 1. Although Braille encoding for all languages share the same Braille font, different languages have different Braille representation rule, thus a single Braille character may be interpreted differently in the context of different languages. Table 1 contains the mapping of same Braille codes to different characters of three different languages: English, Hindi, and Dzongkha.

Braille	English	Hindi	Dzongkha
k	k	क	ཀ
T	.	त	ཐ
" R	" R	ऋ	ར

TABLE 1- Mapping of Braille codes to characters of English, Hindi and Bangla

The Dzongkha script, which is also known as the Bhutanese script, is used to write Dzongkha. The Dzongkha script has 30 consonants and 4 basic vowels. The 30 consonants can occur in three different positions: twice in nominal position and once in orthographic subjoined position (Bhutan, 2004; Tibetan, 2009; Dzongkha, 2005). This leads to a total of 30*3=90 consonants, 4 vowels and 1 extra character, i.e., 95 alphabets in Dzongkha. Therefore, Dzongkha scripts can be written either from top to bottom or from left to right (Bhutan, 2004) (refer to figure 1(b)).

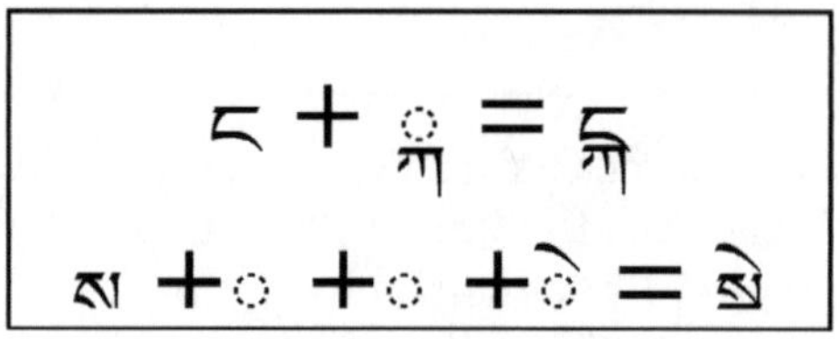

FIGURE 1(A) - Construction of Dzongkha conjugates

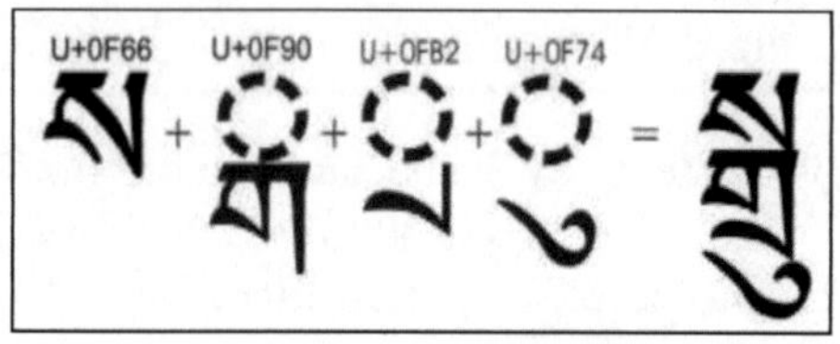

FIGURE 1(B) - Dzongkha chracters arranged from top to bottom

As in other languages, two or more consonants can combine to form a conjugate Dzongkha character. However, these consonants are not separated by any special symbols (as in the case of Indian languages where the consonants within the conjugate are separated by a special symbol called halant). The consonant clustering in Dzongkha takes place between the consonant at the nominal position and consonant at the orthographic subjoined position. This is illustrated in Fig. 1(a). It can be observed from table 2 below that the conjugate characters, as constructed by clustering of consonants and vowels, may have an entirely different visual representation. However, the corresponding transliterated Braille is represented by a sequence of Braille cells for each of the characters.

Rule	Example	Braille
CC	ང + ྐ = ངྐ	@+K
CCV	ང + ྐ + ོ = ངྐོ	GK o
CCC	ས + ྐ + ྱ = སྐྱ	@S@T R
CCCV	ས + ྐ + ྱ + ེ = སྐྱེ	@S@T R9

TABLE 2- Conjugate construction rules with examples taken from Dzongkha language (C=Consonant, V=Vowel)

Unlike any Indian language texts, there exists no inter-word separation in Dzongkha. Each of the Dzongkha words are composed of single or multiple syllables. The syllables are separated by a special symbol called *tsheg*. Each of the syllables contains a root letter, and may additionally contain a prefix, suffix, vowel and post-suffix. Figure 2 illustrates this phenomenon with an example.

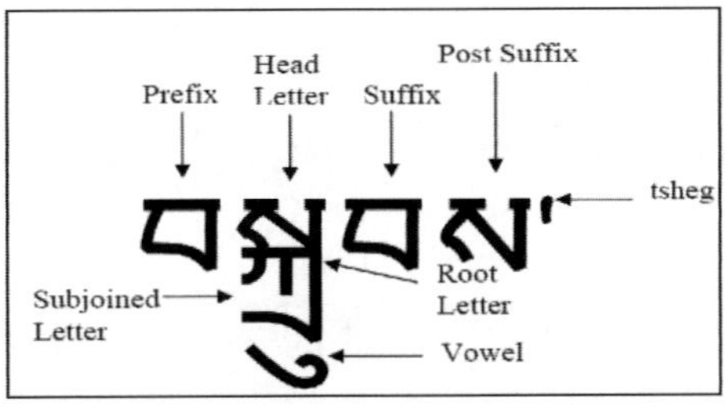

FIGURE 2- Construction of a Dzongkha syllable

4 The System Architecture

The architecture of our proposed Dzongkha text to Braille transliteration (DLBT) system is shown in figure 3. The diagram presents the essential components of the system. The details are discussed in the subsequent sections.

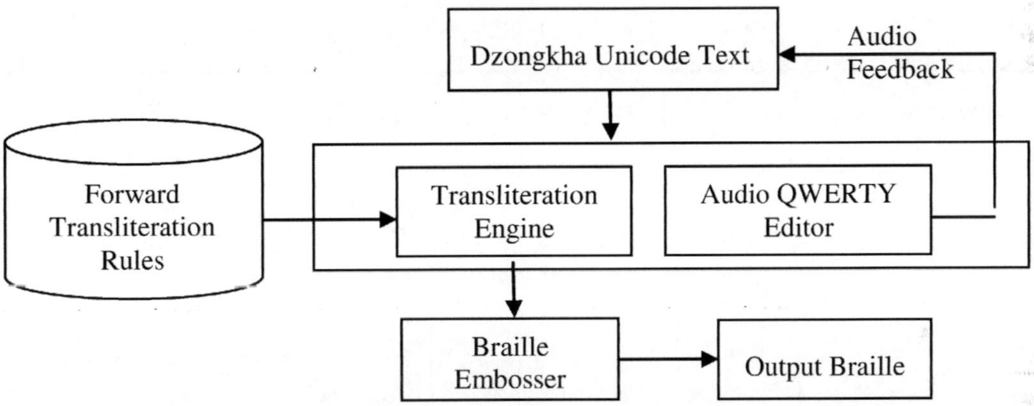

FIGURE 3 - The proposed system architecture

4.1 The Input and Output of the System

The input to the system can either be a Unicode (Hudson, 2000) supported Dzongkha text document written in any popular word processor, or Dzongkha texts entered through a keyboard. Based on the user's requirements, the system can transliterate the given text to Braille. The Braille output is then provided to the Blind user by printing the Braille texts on a large variety of commercially available Braille embossers (Taylor, 2000; Brailler). The current system has been evaluated on the Braille embossers like, Index Basic-S, Index Basic-D, Index 4X4 PRO, Romeo and Juliet Pro.

4.2 Forward Transliteration

Based on the information discussed in section 3, we have constructed distinct forward transliteration rules for Dzongkha text to Braille. The transliteration engine consists of a *code table* which is nothing but a collection of the transliteration rules. An example of the code table structure is shown in figure 4.

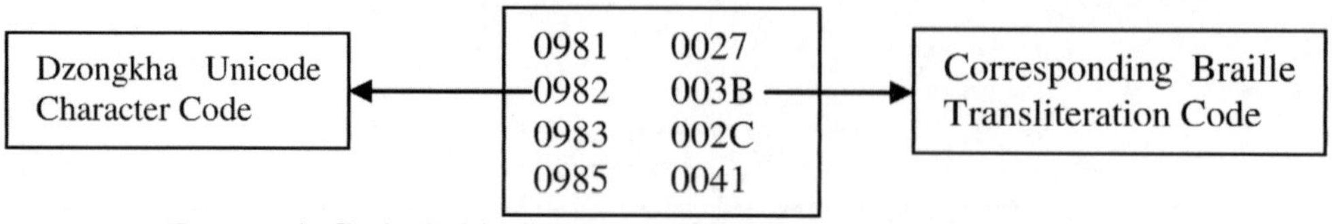

FIGURE 4- Code Table Structure of Forward Transliteration Engine.

Most of the transliteration rules are very similar to Indian language text to Braille transliteration (Lahiri et al., 2005; Dasgupta and Basu, 2009). However, there are few exceptional cases like, handling of some special conjugates in Dzongkha script, where the transliteration rules changes. For example, Braille representation of certain Dzongkha characters like "ra", "la" and "sa" depends upon the occurrence of the character that follows it. This process is represented by the following rule in figure 5:

```
CONJ {PREFIX {U+0f62|U+0f63|U+0f66, U+0f90|U+0F92|U+0F94}}
            → PutBraille (53|59|57)
```

FIGURE 5- Context dependent text to Braille conversion rule in Dzongkha

The rule says, if the head letter of a Dzongkha conjugate begins with U+*0f62*, U+*0f63* or U+*0f66* and the root latter belongs to U+*0f90*, U+*0F92*, or U+*0F94* then the Braille representation of the head characters will changed to "53", "59" or "57". Figure 6 illustrates the above rule with an example; figure 7 shows a screenshot of the working of the Dzongkha text to Braille transliteration system.

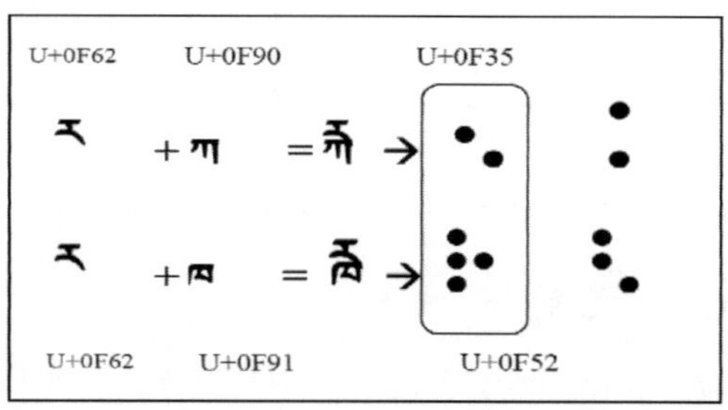

FIGURE 6- Illustration of the context dependent forward transliteration rules in Dzongkha

The Dzongkha Braille transliteration tool allows 38 characters per line and 25 lines per page. However, the system allows the user to change the configuration if needed. As mentioned above Dzongkha script does not allow any inter word space. However, the syllables and sentences are separated by the special symbols: *tsheg* and *she.* An interesting feature found in Dzongkha Braille formatting is that, each line of a Braille document must end with either *tsheg* or *she*. This issue is handled by an inbuilt auto formatting module of the transliteration system. The module first analyses the transliterated Braille output and puts 38 Braille characters per line at the preview window. If the last character of a line is not a *tsheg* or *she* then the module starts accumulating the previous characters into an array till it gets a *tsheg* or *she.* The array elements are then printed into the next line of the preview window. This results into the fact that after transliteration is over all the lines in the Braille output does not contain 38 characters.

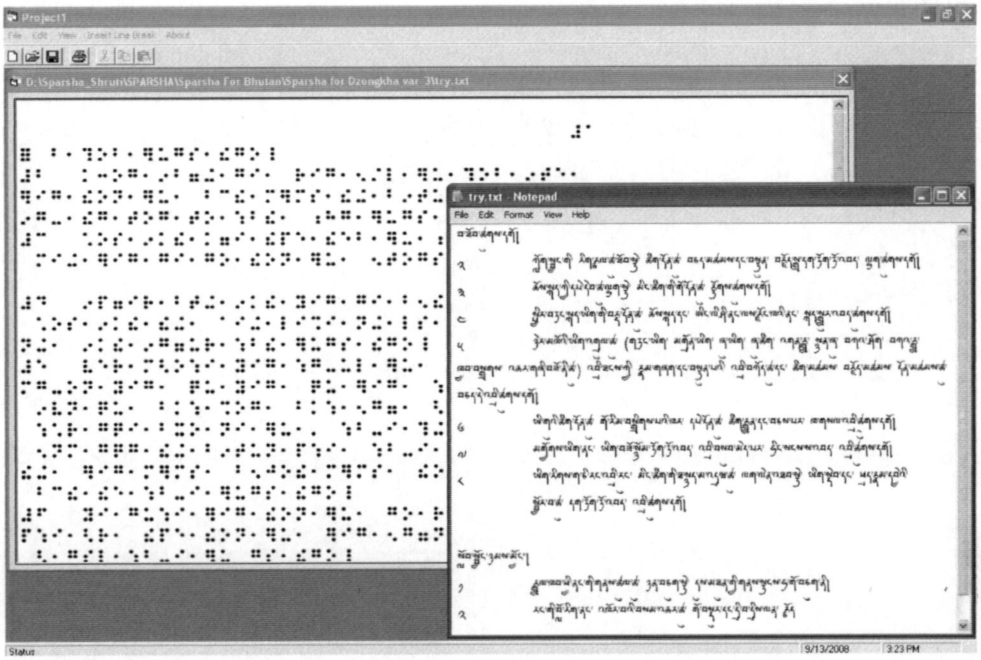

FIGURE 7: WORKING OF THE DZONGKHA TEXT TO BRAILLE TRANSLITERATION SYSTEM

5 Dzongkha Text and Braille Audio QWERTY Editor

The primary goal of the audio QWERTY editor is to allow Blind people to create Dzongkha Text/Braille documents (see figure 8). This requires an interface for accepting the regional language text entered through the keyboard and performing different operations on it, like formatting, printing and saving the text. The creation of a new editor interface was not warranted as it would put additional burden on the user to learn the new system. Hence, we have chosen to use some already existing standard editor with the required capabilities. Our investigations have proved that Microsoft Word can be configured to accept text in regional languages including Dzongkha. Although the Audio QWERTY editor plug-in can be integrated to any other Unicode enabled text editors like, Notepad, and WordPad, the reasons for choosing Microsoft Word are:

1. Support for Unicode– ensures the use of multi-language text documents
2. Rendering of Fonts –uses proper rendering engines for correct rendering of regional language fonts including glyph shaping and repositioning (Rolfe, 2001).
3. Well documented object model – the editor exposes a comprehensive set of objects for interacting with it, this simplifies the task of programming.
4. Ease of Use – the existing popularity of this editor predicts a low learning curve for the proposed system. Further, the editor provides a large number of keyboard-shortcuts.

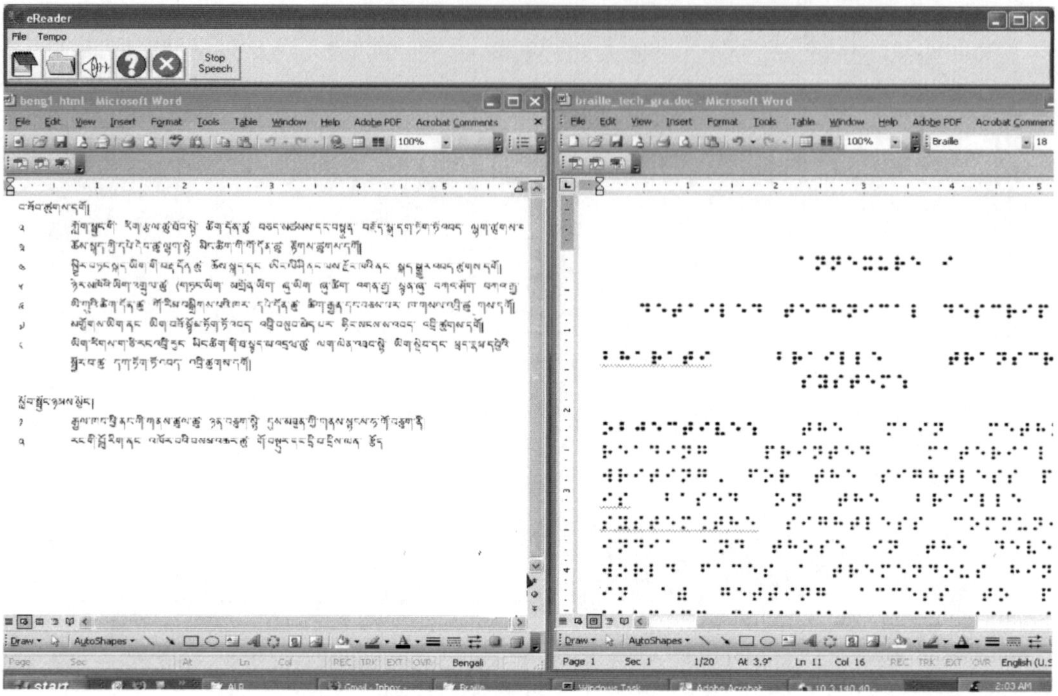

FIGURE 8- The Dzongkha Braille Audio QWERTY Editor. For any key press operation, the Blind user will get audio based feedback.

The audio QWERTY editor is integrated with the pre-recorded Dzongkha alphabet voices that make it different from other commercially available text editor; as a result, each of the keyboard operation performed through this editor is followed by a voice feedback in Dzongkha. This enhances its ease and efficiency for a Blind person to read and write Braille texts.

Conclusion

The Dzongkha text to Braille transliteration system is an attempt to develop low cost technology to assist blind people. The system will help a large segment of Blind population of Bhutan to access printed text book materials. The present version of the system can only perform the forward transliteration of Text to Braille. In future, we will try to incorporate the reverse transliteration approach where given a Braille document it can be transliterated back to its original Dzongkha font. Further, we will provide an online version of the system so that it can be accessed from different parts of the world.

References

A. Basu, S. Roy, P. Dutta and S. Banerjee. "A PC based multi-user Braille reading system for the blind libraries", IEEE Transactions on Rehabilitation Engineering, Vol. 6, No. 1, March 1998, pp.60—68

A. Lahiri, J. S. Chattopadhyay, A. Basu, "Sparsha: A comprehensive Indian language toolset for the blind". Proceedings of the 7th international ACM SIGACCESS conference on Computers and accessibility. 2005.

T. Dasgupta, and A. Basu, "A speech enabled Indian language text to Braille transliteration system", nformation and Communication Technologies and Development (ICTD), 2009, pp-201-211

P. Blenkhorn, "A system for converting Braille to print", IEEE Transactions on Rehabilitation Engineering, Vol. 3, No. 2, June 1995, pp. 215-221

HAL. Dolphin Computer Access, www.dolphinuk.co.uk/products/hal.htm

C.A. Pennington and K.F. McCoy, "Providing intelligent language feedback or augmentative communication users", Springer-Verlag, 1998.

T.V. Raman (1996). "Emacspeak – a speech interface". Proceedings of CHI96, April 1996

winbraille. (n.d.). Retrieved on September 14, 2012, from www.braille.se/downloads/winbraille.htm

Duxbury.(n.d). In Duxbury Braille Translator, 2000. www.duxburysystems.com

indexbraille. (n.d.). Retrieved on September 14, 2012, from www.indexbraille.com

NFBTRANS. National Federation of the Blind, 2004, http://www.nfb.org/nfbtrans.htm

MONTY, VisuAide. http://www.visuaide.com/monty.html

JAWS. 2008. In JAWS for Window. Freedom Scientific. http://www.freedomscientific.com/fs_products/software_jaws.asp

N. Kalra, T. Lauwers, D. Dewey, T. Stepleton and M. B. Dias, "Iterative design of a Braille writing tutor to combat illiteracy", Proceedings of the 2nd IEEE/ACM International Conference on Information and Communication Technologies and Development, December, 2007.

A. Taylor. "Choosing your Braille embosser", Braille Monitor, October 2000. Available at

www.nfb.org/bm/bm01/bm0110/bm011007.htm

Brailler. (n.d). Retrieved from www.brailler.com/

J. Hudson for Microsoft Typography, "Windows glyph processing: an open type primer", November 2000,

http://www.microsoft.com/typography/glyph%20processing/intro.mspx

R. Rolfe, 2001, "What is an IME (Input Method Editor) and how do I use it?" http://www.microsoft.com/globaldev/handson

Bhutan. (2004). downloaded from http://www.tcllab.org/events/uploads/pema-bhutan.pdf

Tibetan. (2009). In The Online Encyclopedia of Writing Systems and Languages, Retrieved October 14, 2009, from http://www.omniglot.com/writing/tibetan.htm

Dzongkha (2005), Retrieved from http://www.learntibetan.net/grammar/alphabet.htm

N.C. Loaber, "Modified standard office equipment for Braille translation and embossing", ACM SIGCAPH Computers and the Physically Handicapped, Issue 21, November 1976, Pages 9-19

Walter J. Weller, Virginia C. Klema, "A rapid Braille transliteration technique for certain IBM machine", Communications of the ACM, Volume 8 Issue 2, Feb. 1965, Pages 115-116

Invited Talk:

Quillpad Multilingual Predictive Transliteration System

Ram Prakash H
Tachyon Technologies P Ltd, Bangalore, India
ramprakash@tachyon.in

ABSTRACT

Transliteration has been one of the common methods for multilingual text input. Many earlier methods employed transliteration schemes for defining one to one mapping of input character combinations to output character combinations. Though such well defined mappings made it easier to write a transliteration program, the end user was burdened with learning the mappings. Further, though transliteration schemes try to map the character combinations phonetically, it is unavoidable to introduce non intuitive combinations into the scheme. An alternative is to use predictive transliteration, where user can input a word, by intuitively combining the input alphabet phonetically and the predictive transliteration system correctly converts it to the target language. This paper presents the challenges that must be addressed to build such a system, and describes how Quillpad can be trained for performing predictive transliteration between any two scripts.

KEYWORDS : transliteration, predictive text input, multilingual text input, Quillpad, decision trees

1 Introduction

Predictive transliteration has proven to be an effective method for text input of Indian languages. This paper discusses general challenges involved in building a practical predictive transliteration system. Further, it describes the key aspects of Quillpad multilingual transliteration system that pioneered such an input method for Indian languages. Though the techniques employed in developing Quillpad system are illustrated in the context of English to Hindi transliteration, the system is generic and can be directly applied to train a system for transliterating between any two alphabet-based languages. Quillpad itself has been successfully trained for phonetic transliteration between Roman input and 16 Indian languages (including Urdu) and Arabic.

The content of this paper will be organised as follows. Section 2 will talk about specific challenges to be addressed by a phonetic transliteration system. Section 3 will discuss the Quillpad system and describe the approaches behind its key modules. Section 4 will briefly discuss some of the issues that have not been addressed by current Quillpad system and can provide some topics for future work.

This document assumes the input language as Roman alphabet and output language as Hindi. Other language examples are used wherever it is appropriate to highlight challenges that may be specific to those languages.

2 Predictive Transliteration Challenges

Predictive transliteration systems should allow users to type in phonetically, by intuitively composing letters from an input alphabet. For the sake of illustration, consider transliterating from Roman alphabet to Hindi. This is an important use case as almost all computers shipped in India come with a Roman keyboard. Predictive transliteration enables users to type in their own language. The following sections highlight the challenges involved in building an effective transliteration solution.

2.1 Phonetic Mapping Ambiguities

Rigid transliteration schemes use upper case and lower case letters to represent similar but different sounds, which generally makes the typing interface cumbersome for the end users. For better usability, the input should be assumed case insensitive. Given this design decision, there are 26 letters in Roman alphabet and 50+ different letters in Hindi. This naturally leads to ambiguous mappings. For example, letter 'd' will be used to represent both 'द' (this) , 'ड'(did) and 'ड़'. Another example is the letter 'n'. 'n' can be used by the user to write 'ञ' , 'ण' (used in Marathi), 'न'(not) and nasal markers like 'ं' (bindu) and 'ँ' (chandrabindu). Phonetic transliteration system should correctly convert the input character to the corresponding Hindi character depending on the word that is being written. Other cases include different Roman letters mapping to a same Hindi character, cluster of Roman characters mapping to a single Hindi character etc.

2.2 Loosely Phonetic Nature

Though Indian languages are generally phonetic, there are cases where one cannot assume strict phonetic nature. This problem is more evident in Hindi. For example, the word 'बचपन' is pronounced as 'bachpan'(IPA: 'bətʃpən') and not as 'bachapana' which would be the pronunciation if the language were to be strictly phonetic. In Hindi, the final consonant is pronounced without the inherent schwa, though the consonant is written with the implicit vowel sound 'ə'. South Indian languages like Kannada, Tamil, Telugu do not follow this rule. Though the rule for handling the final consonant is easy to specify, the challenge is in handling the case where vowel sound 'ə' is skipped in the middle of the word. In the above example, though the word is written as 'ba cha pa na' in Hindi, user would type the word as 'bachpan', as per the pronunciation of the word. In general, when two consonants come together, they should be combined into a conjunct ligature. However, in this case though 'ch' and 'p' are adjacent without any explicit vowel in the input, they should not be combined to form the conjunct 'च्प'. If the Roman input, 'bachpan', is interpreted to be strictly phonetic, the output should have been 'बच्पन' which is not what the user intends to write. This condition can't be defined as the application of this rule is fairly complex and can appear at multiple locations in a given word.

Other extreme cases of this loose phonetic nature can be observed in Arabic and Urdu, where in the output language the vowel sounds are optional in many cases. However, the vowels are explicitly written in the input word as the pronunciation of the word would have the vowel sounds.

2.3 Multiple Input Variants

As a result of issues discussed in 2.1 and 2.2, and other scenarios discussed below, different users can type a given word with multiple variants of input spellings. This problem is compounded by local conventions for writing certain letters or syllables, influence of the native language of the input alphabet and the pronunciation differences due to user's own native tongue influence. Some of these issues are briefly discussed here.

2.3.1 Phonetic Variants

These are generally due to the issues discussed in 2.1 and 2.2. For illustration, consider a Hindi word राष्ट्रपति (IPA: rɑ:ʃtrpət̪ɪ). Users can write any of the following Roman inputs for writing this word. 'rashtrapati', 'rashtrapathi', 'raashtrapathy', 'raashtrpati' etc. All these inputs should yield the correct Hindi word राष्ट्रपति.

2.3.2 Native Language Influence

The native language of the user plays a significant role in determining the phonetic spelling they come up with for writing a word in their language. For example, a Tamil speaking user wanting to write in Tamil is likely to type the input as 'pirakash' for writing 'பிரகாஷ்' (IPA: prəkɑ:ʃ). Most other users would type 'prakash' as input. This is because of how the conjuncts are written in native Tamil words. There are many such local language influences that an effective transliteration system should allow to be incorporated into.

2.3.3 Foreign Language Influence

Users fluent in English may use some spelling conventions that are common in native English words. Such combinations are not phonetic, but many of those combinations are commonly used. For example the Hindi word हम(IPA: həm). Though the phonetic input for this word is 'ham', uses familiar with English might type in 'hum' as input. However, if 'hum' is interpreted phonetically, it would result in 'हुम', which is not the intended output. This is a simple example, but there are many more cases where native English spellings can influence user's input.

2.3.4 Conventional Spellings

There are local conventions for representing certain sounds in regional languages. These conventions have been traditionally set in because of multiple reasons. One, when the local language character does not have any character in English that closely represents its sound. For example 'zh' in Tamil and Malayalam is used to represent sounds that are actually not pronounced as 'z'(IPA). Two, historically certain names are written with spellings that do not faithfully represent its phonetic form in the Indian languages. Consider the name 'Krishnaiah', which is actually represented as 'Krishnayya' in Indian languages. One can find many such examples.

2.4 Multiple Output Words

While previous sections discussed about the variants in inputs, it is also possible for a given input word to have multiple valid outputs. Transliteration system should be able to suggest all those possibilities.

2.5 Transliteration of Foreign Words

It is quite common for the users to type native English words in the middle of their Hindi sentences. As the input alphabet they use is same as the alphabet used for English language, they would naturally enter native English spelling for the word. Most of these spellings firstly, are not phonetic, secondly, do not really represent any native Hindi words. A good transliteration system should allow the users to type native English spellings, and if detected as an English word, should convert it into regional language using English pronunciation of the word. This feature significantly improves user experience as it contributes to fluency in writing in local languages. However, it should be kept in mind that native English pronunciations when represented in Indian language scripts, do not capture the local pronunciation of those words. So, it is important for the transliteration system to convert the native English words into a pronunciation that is acceptable locally, and further use the language specific conventions for representing native English phones.

3 Quillpad System Description

Quillpad transliteration system effectively addresses most of the above mentioned challenges. The solution has been live on www.quillpad.in since 2006. This section briefly discusses the overall approach behind the Quillpad system.

3.1 Overview of the Approach

Quillpad has been designed by modelling the core transliteration task as a multi-class classification problem. It can be trained to transliterate between any two alphabet-based languages. The rough mappings between the alphabet code points of input and output languages is definable using a simple language definition file. Once that is done, rest of the pipeline is automatic. The learning and prediction modules do not assume anything specific to the language pair and almost all the language specific issues mentioned above are completely definable in the external language definition file. Once the definition file is ready, which normally takes 8-10 hours to perfect, the predictive transliteration rules are learned given just the target language corpus, without requiring any sort of parallel transliteration corpus. The prediction itself is just a decision tree traversal for each of the input characters and the words are combined and ordered using a language model. Brief descriptions of these steps are given below.

3.2 Alphabet Mapping Definition

Language definition file that defines the mapping between input and output alphabet character is a simple, regular expression based set of rules to specify what English characters users are likely to use for a given Hindi character. By allowing regular expression models, these options can be controlled and many language specific conventions and transliteration rules can be easily captured. The rules themselves are defined per target character, independent of any word the character would appear in. Thus, defining them does not require deep linguistic expertise and the mappings can be one to many, many to one, and many to many. It must be noted that language definition does not define any rule for actually determining which output character a given input character would be converted to. These are defined per character, and theoretically can be just a dump of all possible input alphabet combinations that a user may enter to type the given character. However, doing so increases the artificial training data exponentially. This point will be further clarified in the next section. Modelling the possible input characters for a given Hindi character, in a context-specific manner, will give the model expressive power to incorporate language specific nuances.

3.3 Training Data Generation

One of the important aspects of Quillpad transliteration system is that it doesn't require a manually prepared transliteration parallel corpus. The alphabet mapping rules are used to generate several possible ways in which the user may type a Hindi word from the corpus. For each Hindi character, the language definition file defines possible English characters the user may use to type it. Such candidates for each Hindi character are combined together to produce multiple possible inputs for a given word. The context specific rules in the language definition model allows one to define rules that would select different candidate English character combinations for a given Hindi character depending on, say, whether that character appears at the beginning of the word, middle of the word, is followed by a particular consonant etc. This controls both the quality and the number of options generated for each corpus word. This significantly determines the quality. Using the English input options generated for every corpus word, one to one correspondence parallel training data is generated.

3.4 Training

Once the training data is generated, a different classifier is trained for each English character. Quillpad uses a decision tree based learning algorithm. The features can be as simple as checking if at a given relative position there is a particular English character. However, it significantly improves the generalisation accuracy of the system if higher level and richer features are used. Some of the higher level features like, if the previous character is a 'consonant', or 'nasal' will prevent the decision tree from splitting on every character as it can be split by checking a condition on a class of characters. For every Hindi character, arbitrary number of these special labels can be assigned in the language definition file. The learning algorithm automatically makes use of those labels to generate these higher level features. Another important aspect for designing the features is to make it invariant to the exact position of the feature in the input string. Quillpad learning algorithm generates such position invariant features, which are independent of any language.

The actual training for a corpus with 5,00,000 unique Hindi words takes about 30-40 minutes. Once the training is complete, it can be used for prediction.

3.5 Prediction

Prediction module takes the decision tree model for each of the input alphabet characters and applies them on every input character independently. The resulting class assignments for each of these characters are combined together to form candidate output words.

3.6 Pre-Processing

Some of the simple issues mentioned in section 2 can be easily handled by pre-processing the input string before passing the input to the prediction engine. Quillpad system makes provision for language specific pre-processing rules. Though this can be addressed by defining appropriate rules in the language definition file, in practice it is more efficient to deal with some of these cases at a pre-processing level.

3.7 Post-Processing

The generation of candidate words as described in 3.5 is restricted by using beam search. Beam search uses the log probabilities returned by the decision trees for determining the words to be trimmed off the list. By incorporating word frequency score during training, the decision tree also serves as a character level language model. This ensures that log probabilities from the trees can be used reliably in the beam search. The candidate lists are further ordered by using a word level language model to present multiple possible output options to the user.

3.8 Dealing with Foreign Words

Quillpad effectively deals with the challenge in handling native English words in the middle of Hindi text. A simple dictionary lookup is used to check if a given word is a valid English word. However, if the given input is also a valid representation of any word in the corpus, it is not considered as a foreign word. Since the phonetics of English and Indian languages are different, such a simple method works very well. Once the input is determined as an English word, a different prediction model, similar to the one used for Hindi prediction, is used to convert the input into its Hindi representation. A different set of decision trees are used for this purpose as mixing native English pronunciation rules significantly differ from those of Hindi prediction. Training them as separate models helps improve both prediction and generalisation accuracy.

4 Conclusion & Future Scope

Quillpad, multi-lingual predictive transliteration system that is described in this paper, is a generic system that can be trained to predictively transliterate between any two alphabet-based languages. Any new language can be supported within a matter of days. The addition of a new language involves defining the basic mappings between the input and the output language, which in theory can be as simple as specifying all the possible ways of representing an output character in input alphabet. However, context specific modelling is supported to have more control on incorporating language specific knowledge. The key idea here is to use thus defined simple language model to generate transliteration parallel corpus for training the prediction module. An AJAX based, rich text editor using the Quillpad technology is available for free use on www.quillpad.in .

Quillpad is the leading solution for Indian language input method online. However, there are a few open issues that are not handled at present by the Quillpad system. Though the current system is very good for most practical scenarios, it does not predict colloquial language well. Since Indian languages are generally phonetic, multiple different dialects and phonetically similar versions of a given word are accepted in written form. This, while rules out dictionary based approaches (See the blog entry for details: http://blog.tachyon.in/2012/03/02/does-quillpad-use-dictionary-for-prediction/), also poses another challenge. Most of the available corpus does not contain the colloquial word forms. Thus, for such words the transliteration would depend only on the generalisation performance of the system. Since a model is not learned on such patterns, the prediction quality is affected. However, it is possible to design a better learning algorithm that can learn to predict the colloquial forms effectively as colloquial forms themselves are some variants of the dictionary form of the word. And the transformation seems to depend mostly on the constraints introduced by our speech production or psycho-acoustic factors. It would be an interesting research topic, though we haven't felt the commercial need for it yet.

Another problem that is not effectively addressed in current Quillpad system is that of transliteration of English words inflected with Indian language suffixes. In South Indian languages, it is quite common to use English words attached with Indian language suffixes. However, the current way of handing Indian language prediction and English word prediction separately, is not the right approach for addressing this issue. A better approach is needed.

Finally, multiple words in Indian languages can be compounded into one word. This scenario is more common with South Indian languages. At the location where two words are joined, the consonants and vowels get replaced or skipped. These changes the local features used for predicting the class of certain characters. This might lead to error in predicted classes for those characters.

Author Index

Association for Computational Linguistics
209 N. Eighth Street
Stroudsburg, Pennsylvania 18360

CURRAN ASSOCIATES INC
proceedings.com